Foundations
in
Polymer
Clay Design

Jay Jones

Barbara A. McGuire

Published by
Krause Publications

700 E. State St. • Iola, WI 54990-0001
715-445-2214
www.krause.com

Please call or write for our free catalog of publications. Our toll-free number to place an order or obtain a free catalog is 800-258-0929 or please use our regular business telephone 715-445-2214 for editorial comment and further information.

Library of Congress Catalog Number 99-61264
ISBN 0-87341-800-X

The following products and companies appear in this publication:
Cernit® (T&F, GmbH); **Creall**®**-therm** (Havo B. V.)**; Gemcolor** (Omyacolor); **Fimo**® modeling material, **Fimo**® *SOFT*, **Fimo Mix Quick, Easy Metal**™, **Fimo**® **pulver, Fimo**® varnish, and **Fimo Puppen** (Eberhard Faber, GmbH); **Sculpey III**®, **Liquid Sculpey, Premo**®, **Sculpey**® **Flex, Sculpey Diluent, Sculpey**™ **Glaze,** and **Super Sculpey**® (Polyform Products, USA); **Claymates**™ (Crooked River, Inc.); **KaleidoKane**™ Designer Canes (Accent Import); **Millefiori Canes, Design Push Molds, Genesis**™ polymer paints, and **Friendly Cutters**™ (Amaco); **Rainbow Wrap**® (Hallcraft, Inc.); **Roll Right**™ Lucite Brayer; **Trattoria**™ Pasta Machines; **Handi chopper**™ (Black & Decker)**; NuBlade**™ kato, **Marxit**™, and **NuFlex**™ kato (Prairie Craft); **Kemper**® pattern cutters, **Kemper**® clay gun, and **Kemper**® clay punches (Kemper Enterprises, Inc.); **Thomas**™ surgical blades (Thomas Medical Supply); **X-Acto**®; **WireForm**® mesh (Paragona™); **Clay Shapers**™ (Forsline & Star Intl. Ltd.); **Feel Good** ™ Bone Folder (SDK Distributors); **Speedball**® linoleum cutters; **Dockyard**™ wood carving tools (Dockyard Model Co.); **Fiskars**® Craft Scissors, **Fiskars**® **Paper Crimper** (Fiskars Inc.); **Kane**™ (Kane Industries Corp); **Wax Floral Cutters** (Stanislaus Imports); **Jasi**™ **Slicer** (Judith Skinner, Inc.); **What A Character**™ **Commotion**®, **the Art of Rubber Stamping**; Running Rhino™ (Uptown Rubber Stamps™, Inc.); **Liquitex**® Artists color (Binney & Smith); **Golden Acrylics**™ (Golden Artist's Colors, Inc.); **Prismacolor**® and **Sharpie**® (Sanford); **Identi**® **pens** and **Pen Touch**™ **Calligraphy metallics** (Sakura); **Magic Leaf**™ (Blattmetall GmbH & Co. KG); **Modern Options**™ **Patinas** (Modern Options, Inc.); **Crafter's Pick**™ Crackling Mediums (API Adhesive Products, Inc.); **Jacquard**™ **Pearlesence powders** (Rupert, Gibbons, Spider); **Gold Leaf**™ **Metallic Powders** (Neuberg-Ebel); **USArtQuest**™ mica flakes (USArtQuest, Inc.); **Wildfiber**™ paper additive (New Basics); **Mini Metallic Rub Ons** and **Decorating Chalks** (Craf-T Products, Inc.); **ArmorAll**™ protectant (Armor All Products Corp.); **Super Glue**™, **Zap a Gap**™, and **E-6000**® silicate glue (Eclectic Product, Inc.); **Artistic**™ **Wire** (Artistic Wire Ltd.); **Coiling Gizmo** (The Refiner's Fire); **Wire Wizard**™ **Mastering the New Clay**™ (Gameplan ArtRanch) **Mindstorm**™ **Productions, abba daba**™ **(**Productions LLC)

*D*edication

To my sons, Robby and Timmy, and Terry McGuire, whom I will always love.

*A*cknowledgments

Diane Dunville

"Night for Day" by Diane Dunville of Illuminart. This exquisite lamp is an example of outstanding design elements and graces the headings throughout this book. Even the smallest portion of good design is a work of art.

"I sent you to reap what you have not worked for. Others have done the hard work and you have reaped the benefits of their labor." John 4:38

To my friends, my peers, my mentors, for their generosity and immense talents.
To Bryan, Ralf, Accent Import, Angela, and Eberhard Faber, for their loyalty, commitment, and ideals.
To Jeanne, Nan, Donna, Kathleen, Amy, Margaret, and Tory for their special attention and care.
To my parents for their infinite giving.
To my church for its discipline, courage, and love, without which I would not be the person I am today.
And to my God who is forever faithful.

On the front cover: "Heart Purse" by Kathleen Dustin; photo by George Post. "Mood Ingido" by Diane Dunville; photo by Dixon Withers Julian. "Egyptian Queen" by Barbara A. McGuire; photo by Don Felton.
On the back cover: "Suspended Wealth Necklace" by Judith Skinner. "African Mask Box" by Kim Korringa; photo by George Post. Kimono by Carol Steinman Zilliacus; photo by Norma Watkins.

Table of Contents

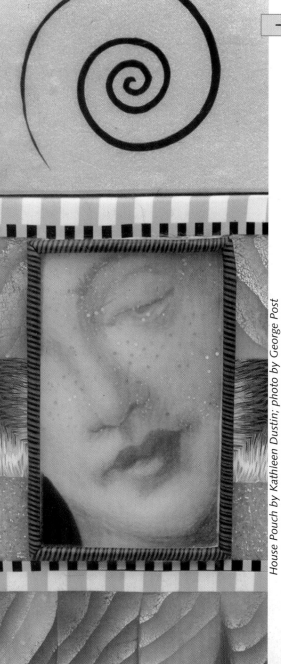

House Pouch by Kathleen Dustin; photo by George Post

Introduction

"Scarab" by Barbara A. McGuire. Inspired by instruction from Cynthia Toops on micro-mosaics, this piece explores the elements and principles of design.

Many years ago I invested hundreds of dollars at a prestigious art academy to learn less is more; but it wasn't until I started to work in polymer clay that the very concepts I had labored over came into appreciative understanding. The current craze surrounding polymer clay, or any new art medium for that matter, may consist initially of a discovery of effects, techniques, and products rather than the expression of an artist. Indeed, it is often easier to design based on the technique itself rather than original composition or use of art elements; however, there are amazing artists who have excelled in their creativity because they have employed good art at its core. Their work is inspirational for expanding the art of polymer clay to its true potential. Good design includes quality of all art elements and principles. In this book, I hope you will learn how to identify these elements and principles and consider how to use them while creating works of art. No longer will you look at a block of clay and wonder, What shall I do with it? Your ideas will have structure long before you even approach preparation, and you will have a firm plat-form on which to expand, discover, and truly create from your own being.

Barbara A. McGuire

PART 1

Understanding Polymer Clay

When an artist wishes to create, *there is always a choice as to which medium is best to give creativity a voice. The work of art and the material it is composed of should complement each other. Polymer clay is a medium that is responsive to many applications and techniques; it has emerged as an incredibly sophisticated, dynamic art medium, brought to life by the creativity and design ability of individual artists. This first section of the book discusses design advantages and limitations of working with polymer clay, general information regarding techniques and basic instruction, as well as a list of materials that are specifically recommended for use with polymer clay. Familiarity with what polymer clay can do will encourage you to discover what you can do with your creative spirit.*

Chapter 1

Appreciating Polymer Clay

For polymer clay to be thoroughly understood, it is perhaps necessary that the beholder be encouraged to view the artwork as a pictorial creation. It is art in miniature. The pendant on a necklace is actually a tiny and total creation of art. It is integrated with a complementary design that allows it to be functional, but the piece itself is appreciated for the design elements within that tiny area. It is as if each composition deserves to be framed and appreciated as an art rendering, not as a "bead" or "pin" entity. Much in the same way enameled jewelry or scrimshaw is appreciated in miniature, polymer clay delights in the scrutiny of small detail. That's not to say that polymer clay cannot go big spatially—quite the contrary.

Michael Grove

Above: "Dancing 2" by Michael Grove. This polymer clay "painting" illustrates the ingenuity and talents of Grove to successfully use the unique properties of polymer clay in a pictorial image.

Left: "The Rescue" by Cynthia Toops. Toops' incredible drawings are rendered in an unbelievable assemblage of micromosaic strips of clay. Her miniature works of art reflect days of meticulous precision and are exclusive one-of-a-kind pieces.

Dan Adams

John Fago

"Elk" by Celie Fago. Not only is the pendant a masterpiece in itself, but the functional aspects of suspending the work is integrated into the design.

Polymer clay is such a richly versatile material that it is the artist who can choose to utilize this medium in any number of formats. But, as in metal smithing, jewelers have the option of creating their art in a small form. To purchase a metal bead, and pay an appropriate price for it, one must appreciate the design in it as well as the process with which it was created; no one buys a metal bead for the minerals in it. The materials themselves are but a catalyst for the art. The same is true for glass, ceramic, paper, wood, or cloth, including canvas. It is the art that makes a Van Gogh valuable, not the pigment in the paint.

Chapter 2

General Instructions and Design Considerations

When you first pick up polymer clay, it has a friendly, playful, responsive feeling. It is easy to get overwhelmed by the potential of the design and become impatient as you are learning the basics; however, your skills will increase the more you practice basic things. This is because the beauty of polymer clay *is* its simplicity. Polymer clay is sheer joy to create with and there are no mistakes! This chapter is a basic overview of information to familiarize you with clay, so that you can discover how to use polymer clay, understand safety recommendations, and be informed of general information and basic techniques before you begin to design. For more information regarding the materials and supplies mentioned in this chapter, please see the following chapter.

Work Surfaces

Preferred work surfaces will reflect the tastes of the artist. A piece of card stock works well as a work surface and can be attached with tape to a tabletop, glass or acrylic, for stability. Some artists work with clay directly on glass or marble, but others may find that such surfaces draw heat from the clay. On non-porous surfaces, a piece of work may stick and require lifting by sliding a blade under the art to release it from the work area. This is particularly true if you work directly on acrylic (you also run the risk of distorting your piece while releasing it from the work surface). At all times the area should be kept clean and clear of scrap clay or foreign particles.

Conditioning

All clays must be conditioned before use. Conditioning means to prepare the clay by aligning the molecules within the clay. This enables the clay to become pliable and stretch. A simple way to condition clay is to knead it by rolling it between your palms. Even a slight difference in body or room temperature will make the clay softer. Roll the clay into a snake, doubling, twisting, and stretching it until it is pliable.

Many polymer clay artists utilize a pasta machine to help with conditioning, mixing color, and preparing clay into sheets. Running clay through the machine is easier on your hands and wrists than kneading it. A method for conditioning clays that are soft in nature, such as Fimo soft, Premo, or Cernit, is to begin by cutting the raw clay into thin slices and running the sliced clay through a pasta machine, folding the clay onto itself and running it through over and over, until the clay is supple and the color, if mixed, is thoroughly blended.

For conditioning large quantities of firm clay such as Fimo classic, it is recommended to use a food processor. Softer clays may not be suitable for this method because the clay tends to get stuck in the blades, preventing the shaft from turning. Small hand choppers are adequate, depending on the amount of clay you wish to process. To condition the clay with this method, slice the clay into small chunks to avoid jamming the motor and chop for approximately 60 seconds. The clay will divide into small pieces and then clump together when it begins to warm through heat and friction. Next, empty it out onto a work surface or piece of waxed paper. Press or roll it into sheets, then send the sheets of clay through a pasta machine to thoroughly diminish air pockets, blend color, and prepare the clay into even sheets of the desired thickness.

New colors can also be mixed during the conditioning process, achieving two goals at once. Creating your own colors of polymer clay is an advantage in design. Unlike natural clays, brilliant pigments are a specific element in the polymer clay formulation and can be blended to achieve any imaginable color (hue), shade, or tint. You can mix the colors in any proportions to invent new colors— all it takes is a little patience. Folding and running the clay through a pasta machine will make the blending of colors easier. Beginning with two colors of clay you can see how they swirl and stretch into marbled patterns until the thin strands of color meld into another color. Flattening a twisted piece of clay will produce thin stripes. Slicing through a colored strand will reveal another dimension of the clay—the surface may look different from the inside, and the way you slice may create an interesting color mix.

Softeners

If you wish to soften clay, you may add a softener produced by the manufacturer. If the softener is a liquid, such as Sculpey Diluent, add just a few droplets to the clay during conditioning. Fimo clay can be softened with Mix Quick, which is a solid. The recommended ratio is no more than one-third Mix Quick to two-thirds clay.

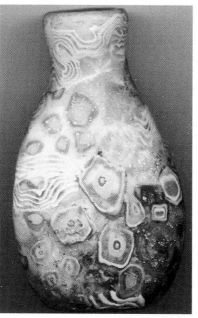

Shauna Poong

Shauna Poong. Creativity comes to life in this vessel which incorporates translucent clay techniques. The extremely thin layers of translucent clay were achieved with the help of a pasta machine.

Many artists also use a few drops of mineral oil (added during conditioning) to soften the clay, even though it is not formulated for this use.

Baking Clay

All clays must be cured by heat (follow the manufacturer's printed instructions). In general, polymer clay cures between 212° and 275° F. Translucent clays are more susceptible to overheating and browning. Clay burns at 350° to 375° F and can emit harmful fumes, so always make sure to bake clay in a ventilated area. Use an oven thermometer to assure even and consistent baking. Baking time is typically 20 to 30 minutes, depending upon the thickness of the piece. Some artists will extend the baking times to assure complete curing of the clay; however, preferences and variables warrant individual testing. It is worth noting that if a piece is not baked at an adequate temperature, the clay will not completely cure and may be brittle.

A home oven will suffice for curing clay in most circumstances, although if you frequently bake polymer clay, it is suggested you invest in a portable toaster or convection oven. Convection ovens are considered to give the best results due to the even heat distribution. Consistent and evenly-distributed heating is an important consideration. It is strongly recommended that you use an oven thermometer to assure accurate baking temperatures.

Clay is hot as it comes out of the oven and must be allowed to cool before handling. Polymer clay hardens as it cools; it first appears rubbery but firms in a few minutes. If you are designing a large, flat surface, you may wish to prevent warping by weighing it with books while it is cooling. Once cured, polymer clay will not shrink and may be drilled, carved, or buffed.

Polymer clay has been tested non-toxic and

packages bear the AP approval seal. In European packaging, this symbol may be different according to European regulations. Although clays are considered non-toxic, they are non-edible and should not be used with food substances or to carry food, or baked together with food. Make sure to clean your oven regularly to avoid any possible residue emitted from the curing (baking) process. Also, polymer clay will not hold water, but perhaps a solution to this may be discovered in the future. Many artists prefer to wear thin latex gloves as they work which protect them from any possible chemical reaction—this also helps keep fingerprints from a finished piece.

Uncured polymer clay may react with other substances such as polyurethane varnish. Polymer clay will "eat" through some PVC plastics or Styrofoam! Never place uncured clay on your computer monitor or VCR case. Raw clay will also leach the plasticizer, drawing an oily residue on paper (although this is sometimes intentional to stiffen the clay).

When storing clay, wrap it in heavy-duty plastic, because ordinary stretch plastic wrap will deteriorate over time. Using tin foil or waxed paper is acceptable but may be hard to release from the clay. Store in a dark, cool place, in an airtight container. Light and heat are the two main things that will harden clay, but if it is stored properly, clay will remain workable for many years.

The recommended baking surface is any heavy card stock or parchment paper placed on a rack or metal baking sheet. It is not recommended to bake directly on glass, because it may accumulate heat, making an accurate temperature reading difficult, and a glass surface is so polished that the clay will also acquire a shiny, smooth surface where it touches the glass. This may or may not be desirable but is very hard to control and usually results in areas with air pockets (especially when baking flat objects). When baking beads or any form other than a flat piece, a slight flatness may occur where the object (especially beads) rests, due to the increased heat and weight in that particular spot. This can be avoided by suspending beads on a wire rod when baking or by using props for odd-shaped or large items. You can be inventive and create your own props and carriers out of wire, paper, or polymer clay. Props such as folded papers (accordion style) or even billows of sheeting have been

used; however, all props must be able to withstand baking temperatures appropriate for polymer clay.

Cleaning Clay

To clean polymer clay, wipe it with a damp cloth. You may wash most clay buttons or beads in warm water and dry in low heat, but polymer clay will not withstand dry-cleaning chemicals. It is very important when designing buttons, or any objects that will be exposed to outdoor weather, that you thoroughly test your choice of clay; some clays may deteriorate under out-of-the-ordinary conditions.

Gluing Clay

Polymer clay may require testing for compatible glues. The perfect, easy-to-use glue for polymer clay is yet to be found. Water-based, hot glues, and "white" glues will simply not stick. Some glues have a "cold snap"; that is, they can snap under weather variations. Two-part epoxy has strength and reliability but must be mixed and applied in a ventilated area. Given the variables, it is advantageous to avoid glue and secure required findings into the designed piece with a swatch of polymer clay before baking. Besides being more predictable, this often adds a finished, creative, more professional look.

Armatures and Strength

Most modeling clays air-dry rigid before firing, but polymer clay does not. Therefore, gravity has an effect on the stability of uncured polymer clay. Forms must be designed with the knowledge that uncured clay cannot provide support for additional weights. This limitation, however, can be remedied by using an armature. For large projects or to ensure stability in flat surfaces, wire mesh is an excellent lightweight, rustproof, woven material that can be embedded into the clay and formed. It comes in varying weaves and metals, including aluminum, brass, copper, and stainless steel. It is very flexible and can be cut with ordinary scissors. Wire aluminum rods are available to strengthen extruding parts.

George Post

"Tower Vase" by Barbara A. McGuire. This vessel was inspired by the artist Klimt and used WireForm mesh in its structure. The mesh supports the arched curves of the form and also strengthens the base.

may be brittle. Recently, clays with increased elasticity have been developed that enable thin strands to flex. Baking practices may also be a deciding factor in the strength of the clay, but the design itself has the most influence in the strength and endurance of a piece. Obviously, the thinner the sheet strand or extrusion, the more vulnerable the piece. It is beneficial to design the art without making the clay susceptible to breaking. As a result of this minor limitation, you may be challenged to solve problems in a creative manner!

Creating with Clay

For most beginners, a natural way to start discovering polymer clay is with modeling. Making characters such as snakes, snowmen, and teddy bears will familiarize you with how soft the clay is. You can also practice stretching and rolling long, even snakes and tiny strands of clay. You will discover how the clay sticks to itself when unbaked, how to smooth the seams, and how much pressure you will need to secure additional pieces. Remember, each brand is different and will have different properties as a modeling material.

Polymer clay is a natural for making beads. Begin by making bead forms in a variety of sizes. These don't have to be round; they can be square, triangular, cylindrical, or oval. To drill a hole, start at one end and twist a needle tool through the bead. When the needle is almost completely through, reverse the bead and poke the opposite end from where you started. This eliminates a protrusion at the bead hole. It is also a good idea to bake the beads "hole side" down, so if there is a "flat spot" it is near the hole. Beads can also be baked on a suspended wire. To make even-sized beads, roll a snake and slice into even lengths. You can then shape the individual beads as desired.

Tin foil is also a common armature for developing a form. Glass, wood, and paper forms are appropriate as long as those materials are able to withstand the oven temperatures required to cure the clay. Glass and metal forms may be covered with clay, but acrylic and Styrofoam are not suitable because they cannot withstand the required heat. Some forms will not serve as an armature until the surface has been prepared to accept the clay. This is true of papier mâché forms: coat the paper armature with a layer of Sobo Glue, let dry, and proceed to cover with polymer clay.

Once properly cured, polymer clay has a good degree of strength. Certain clays may retain some flexibility, whereas other clays

"Hawaii" by Christine Alibert-Mas. Alibert-Mas has creatively found a way to hold the form of these colorful loop beads without comprising their strength.

Jean-Luc Mas

Graduated size beads are made by slicing an even cylinder in graduated lengths (for example, 1", 3/4", 1/2", and 1/4" lengths).

Cutting Clay

Using polymer clay as a base to decorate has many possibilities. You may wish to try creating a pin, barrette, or magnet. You can experiment with a cookie cutter shape or you can also use a blade to trim a freeform design. Small knives with detachable blades are commonly used to cut clay. For clean cuts through large units of clay, an extremely sharp blade called a tissue blade should be used. Tissue blades, which are professional surgical blades used in the medical industry, must be used with caution at all times. Recently, blades have been developed particularly for polymer artists. Rigid blades are great for slicing straight edges and canes, while blades that are flexible enable cutting smooth curves.

Rolling Clay

An acrylic brayer or a thick glass cylinder will help flatten sheets of clay and smooth surfaces. The clear quality of acrylic allows you to see your work and the clay won't stick to the surface (although it will stick to wood). Cut acrylic dowels will also work well and are inexpensive. A pasta machine, however, is the most invaluable tool, not only for conditioning but also for making thin sheets. The roller setting will determine the thickness of the sheet. Recently, many artists have purchased motors that attach to the machine which enable them to hold the clay while it passes through the machine.

Texture

Polymer clay accepts texture and serves as a mold-making element; virtually anything can be pressed into polymer clay. Fabric, rubber stamps, jewelry findings, spoon handles—anything with texture will work. You can even press a doll's face into the clay! Just be sure to use a release powder, such as cornstarch, to prevent the item from sticking.

To duplicate items, forms, or texture, you can make a mold using the clay itself. First, take a portion of clay large enough to accept what you

Cheryl Darrow, copyright Running Rhino & Co. This image produced by Uptown Rubber Stamps was pressed into polymer clay, colored, and split into several sections to make an interesting wall piece.

are "molding." Coat your item with a release powder and press it into the clay. Pull the soft clay up around the sides of the object if it is a deep form. Release the object without distorting the clay mold. Bake the mold. You now have a mold which you can use for duplication. Buttons, dolls, beads, and broaches—all can be made of polymer clay using a polymer clay mold! Simply press clay (with release powder) into your mold and remove carefully. There are also commercial molds available in flowers, fruits, bears, angels, and more.

Rubber stamps are an essential means of impressing an image (as well as letters) into polymer clay. Stamps have also been used for creating texture and patterns. Personalized images or script can be made into stamps. Many rubber stamp companies have now become known as "angel companies" because they allow an artist to use an image (provided it is not licensed) as an element in the artist's own creation. Before proceeding to sell art with rubber stamp images, make sure to check with the manufacturer to verify that you have followed copyright regulations.

Carving Clay, Surface Decoration, and Altering the Look

Clay can be carved both wet or dry. This can be done with a pencil and tracing paper: draw the image on a piece of tracing paper, place it on the clay, outline it with a pencil, and remove the paper. A slight indentation will appear that can be deepened with a ball-point tool. Carving can also be done with a linoleum cutter or wood-carving tool after the clay is baked. The carved lines may be filled with paint to distinguish the grooves. The paint can be dark or light, depending upon the design choice.

Additional clay pieces, both baked or unbaked, can be applied to the surface for additional decoration. If the pieces are already baked, it is recommended to coat the baked clay with a layer of Sobo Glue to assure proper bonding. This also is true for non-polymer applied objects that can go in the oven. You can embed the object into the surface. If you wish to try a frame with an applied mosaic border, the mosaics are baked on first and then a "grout" of softer clay is pushed into the crevices and baked. Liquid softener, used sparingly, can also aid in adhering applied clay pieces.

The surface can be colored or shaded with powders that are mica, pearl, or metallic. Metallic powders are brilliant but must be used with a dust mask; take caution not to inhale the particles. There is a natural adhesion when powders are spread on a clay's surface. They are applied in small quantities with a Q-tip, soft brush, or cloth. All powders should be varnished after baking to prevent rubbing off in areas exposed to wear. Clay manufactures produce varnishes especially formulated for polymer clay in both matte and gloss finishes.

Available in composite leaf, hand-burnished patterned leaf, and real gold leaf, metal leaf is beautiful as a surface treatment. Once you apply the leaf directly onto raw clay, it sticks by itself. If you then separate or stretch the clay the leaf will separate into tiny crackles, depending on how you stretch it. Running a clay sheet with gold leaf through a pasta machine will give you an evenly dispersed crackle. As with powders, leaf should be varnished to protect the final finish.

"Anasazi Spirits" by Patricia Weller of Morning Dove Designs. Weller uses a technique of original impressed images and metal leaf to create a mysterious effect.

Barbara A. McGuire. This pin was made with Creative Clay Stamps, translucent and metallic clays, and metallic powders.

Heat transfer foils are attached to a plastic release paper, transferred to the clay, and heat set in baking. Be sure to place the gray side of the foil on the clay when applying. The plastic can be peeled off after baking. These foils come in a multitude of bright colors, some with holographic effects. They require experimentation before use to achieve the desired results.

Clay can also be painted or antiqued to make it look ancient. Acrylic paint is recommended, because the chemicals in oil paints may react with the clay. Paint is popular to define carving. To do this, paint the entire surface and then wipe with a soft cloth while the paint is still wet. You can also allow the paint to dry and then wet-sand the raised surfaces. Images or patterns can also be silk-screened onto the clay. Surface patterns can be screened in multiples to create a more complex composition. Acrylic interference paint is also popular to use with screened pattern designs.

Baked polymer clay can be drawn on with colored pencils. Sculpey white and Fimo soft white are excellent bases for this technique. In addition to drawing directly on clay, you can trace or draw an image using colored pencils on a sheet of tracing paper and later transfer the image to the clay. You can also color machine-copied images with colored pencils and transfer the colored image.

Transferring copy machine images, either black and white or color, to clay is very easy. To transfer an exact image, you will need to machine copy images onto transparency film (especially if you are transferring type), because the mirror image will be transferred to the clay. Straight transfers will produce a "flipped" image. Individual copier machines may produce different results due to the inks used (which are actually polymers) and the quality of the reproduction. To transfer, simply place the copier machine image's ink side to the clay. Rub firmly to eliminate gaps or air bubbles. Rubbing alcohol can be (but is not absolutely necessary) spread on the backside of the paper to help the ink release onto the clay. If left overnight, the clay will grab the ink, or you can bake the clay with the paper attached and peel it free after it is cool. Any trace of paper left on the clay after baking can be dissolved with water and peeled off. It is popular to design clay borders around transferred images, in particular pictures you have drawn and reduced.

"Pug Dogs" by Linda Bernstein. Bernstein uses her original pen and ink drawings of pug dogs as transfers in her designs.

Borrowed from Japanese artists, a wood layering technique called mokume gane is popular to use as a surface embellishment. This is a method of layering thin sheets of clay and then altering, impressing, or distorting the stack of layers. Then the clay is "shaved" by removing thin slices with a tissue blade. The exposed layers reveal incredible shapes of color and patterns. Try stacking several layers of very thin clay (especially gold leaf underlying translucent clay) and distort the layers by poking objects into the stack, from the top or bottom. This can be a straight edge, a ball-tip tool, the blunt end of cookie cutters, or even balls of clay placed on the underside. Compact the stack and roll the surface slightly to compress it so there are no gaps, or, if desired, plan on gaps in the slices—both methods are interesting. Shave thin slices from the surface by skimming the very top of the stack horizontally with a tissue blade. The removed slices are then used to decorate surfaces of clay beads, flat clay shapes, or clay forms. One of the most beautiful and popular techniques of mokume gane is a variation where extremely thin layers of pastel-tinted translucent clay and gold leaf are stacked, distorted, and then sliced to reveal the resulting "waves" of gold surfacing through the layers.

Surface treatments for polymer clay are infinite. As you discover each one, you will gain a variety of techniques to use with your design abilities. Many artists combine several techniques in one piece. To say the least, polymer clay is user-friendly and invites experimentation!

Clay generally bakes to a matte finish, but it can also be buffed to a high glossy shine. First, wet-sand the art (by hand) in progression of 400, 600, and 800 grit wet sand papers. Then use a jeweler's buffing wheel with a soft pad to polish the surface. If you don't have a machine, you can buff by hand using something as ordinary as a pair of jeans!

You can alter the look of polymer clay by adding foreign objects such as glitter, crayons, micas, and even herbs. These can be mixed into the clay, particularly translucent clay, to create an infinite variety of effects, including simulated stone. Simple forms and sculptures, as well as large surface areas, may benefit from the interest of an "invented" clay. As always, when altering the clay, you must test to assure your "invention" is appropriate and safe for its intended use.

It has recently been discovered that metallic clays, cut or impressed at certain angles, are able to create an illusion of depth. Small mica particles within the clay reflect and absorb light, making the particles appear as different values of color. Depending on the angle the clay is altered, it will have a shimmering light value or slightly darker value. The subtle contrast gives the illusion of a difference in color and value, and subsequently, depth. This illusion of depth is so effective that the surface appears to be three-dimensional. Application of this quality is a relatively new emergence in polymer clay art. Experiments with canes, stamps, applied pieces, and carvings have produced very interesting results (see the project Less is More, page 130). Once the surface is altered, it is again rolled flush, sanded, and buffed. The illusionary depth emerges from the polished surface. This is a perfect example of how an artist's curiosity often drives the discovery of a new technique and its resulting application in design.

George Post

Pier Voulkos and Dan Peters. A genius of design, Voulkos pioneered the use of the mica shift in clay. Together with the exceptional woodworking talents of Dan Peters, Voulkos has leaped into another dimension in polymer clay: incredible veneered forms.

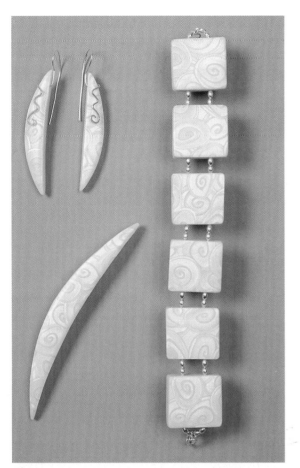

Debbie Krueger. Inspired by Pier Voulkos, Krueger uses the mica shift to subtly enhance her jewelry set.

Millefiori glass canes. (The word Millefiori is an Italian word meaning "thousand flowers.") The original Millefiori canes were developed by Italian glassmakers who assembled rods of glass together to make a design, pulled the glass canes to a small diameter, and then sliced the canes into disks. The tiny pieces were assembled with molten glass to decorate fine glass vessels or beads. This technique is commonly used in design with polymer clay art because the clay has incredible reduction qualities, while still holding the design and color in place.

An artist must make effective choices in design to reduce canes with crisp definition and harmony of color; otherwise, the eye will blend the colors of the clay to gray and the spatial relations will disappear—and interest is lost. But, if contrast is achieved, miniature scale is a unique design element the artist can utilize. Achieving definition and clarity in a design, as well as the control that eliminates distortion, comes from knowing the nature of individual clays. The most opaque clays offer distinction in contrast while transparent clays will blend, creating a shaded

TBF assorted cane slices from Edwin. These beautiful images and borders reflect the ability of the artists of Two Bent Fish to use value and contrast in defining the design.

Canes

Perhaps the most amazing property of polymer clay is its ability to stretch, reduce, and retain the color and proportion of assembled shapes. A skilled artist can assemble the clay to create images of flowers, faces, stars, or any pattern desired. The stack or rod is called a cane, as in

Michael Grove. Thin clay slices hold their form to create these precise and beautiful works of art. The repetitive use of cane creates unity and rhythm, as well as balance.

effect. Some clays are firmer and hold the shape of the cane while softer clays may smear the design as you slice. Some clays are difficult to stretch and tend to break apart. All of the clay within the cane should be the same consistency in softness in order to reduce properly.

To experiment with canes, begin with a simple jelly roll cane. Place two sheets of clay on top of each other. Wedge the borders so the clay will roll smoothly together. Roll the sheets of clay into a cylinder. This cane is one of the most stan-

dard and popular motifs in polymer clay design. Combinations of colors and thickness of layers are infinite. Once assembled, the roll can be shaped into a square or triangle.

Slicing the cane may require a little practice. On round canes, rolling as you slice will keep the cane round. If the cane is square, rotate it between slices to assure even pressure. If the clay is too soft it can be placed in a refrigerator or allowed to set overnight. Reduce a round cane by rolling it evenly on a flat surface; use both hands working from the middle to the outside. If you pinch the ends of a cane, it may reduce the distortion because the outer layers have a tendency to envelope around the middle. Change directions often, and even flip the cane from time to time; this compensates for twisting that may occur by continuous pressure in any one direction. Reduce a square cane by rolling the top and bottom with a brayer, rotating sides frequently to avoid uneven pressures that may distort the design. Again, flip the cane and change directions to help assure the evenness of pressure. This is an important consideration when you are making a face and want the proportions to remain relative. Many a face has resulted in a twisted expression!

Once the cane is finished, you may use the

Above: "Egyptian Queen" by Barbara A. McGuire. Cane reduction depends on the ability of the clay to hold a design. This cane was reduced by utilizing two glass disks to pull the middle of the cane.

Above Left: "Japanese Lady Geisha and Kabuki Man" by Janet Farris. The details in these fine Japanese portraits are reduced in nearly perfect proportion.

slices to decorate a surface, like raw or baked clay, glass, prepared wood, or paper, or you can also make beads directly out of sliced portions of cane by slicing the cane into an even thickness and piercing a hole lengthwise through the bead. The positioned slices of a cane can cover a large surface area with a pattern motif or connect purposefully to create an even more intricate pattern. The ability to repeat the image or connect a pattern allows the artist to frame or border compositions with amazingly intricate design. Rich floral patterns, precise geometric designs, Celtic knot work, measured accurate checkerboards, simple striping, and zigzags can all be produced by the repetition of cane work. Individual slices of cane can also add a textural element to design, as well as a decorative element.

Pre-made canes are also available which enable crafters to experiment, discover, and learn

Resources for the Artist

More than fifty titles have been written regarding projects, techniques, and information relating to polymer clay. These range from pamphlets on miniatures and children's crafts to incredible articles by prestigious magazines such as *Ornament* and *American Craft*. The most current information is presented by the National Polymer Clay Guild, its newsletter, and website, and includes lists of shows and classes occurring throughout the country. Many of the individual artists featured in this book teach classes and sell their work individually and through galleries. The Internet newsgroup **rec.crafts.polymer-clay** has played a definite role in answering questions from beginners, providing information regarding supplies, and sharing the results of experiments regarding techniques and applications. An Internet swap network at Polymer Clay Central (on Delphi) has encouraged artists to share their knowledge by trading art based on a particular theme. National conferences and retreats held throughout the year have allowed artists to meet each other and become friends through sharing information and creating art. Polymer clay has become not only a dynamic art medium but a delightful social interest.

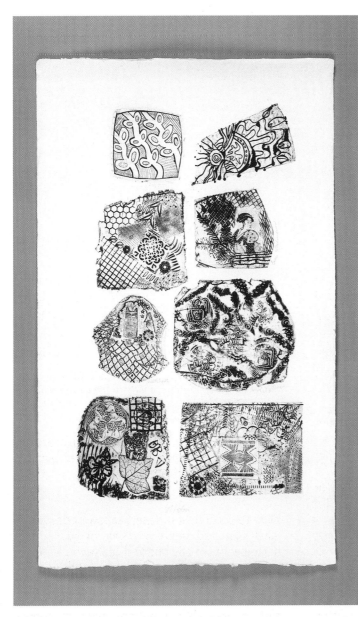

"Intaglio Print" by Maggie Ashton. This lovely print was created at Making History, a conference sponsored by the National Polymer Clay Guild. The conference experimented with new techniques such as printing from blocks made of polymer clay.

Presentation and Craftsmanship

The quality of a work relies on craftsmanship, as well as the design of the piece. This is imperative for the acceptance of polymer clay as a fine craft medium. Sloppy work discredits the artists who have continually striven to gain acclaim in prestigious galleries. Practice will increase your skill, but your goal should always be to produce clean, precise, and durable art—corners should match, edges should be finished,

about applying canes before investing time and clay in creating original canes. These purchased canes are usually icons that can be reduced and enhanced by additional borders, thereby challenging the crafter to incorporate the cane into an overall design that is original. The important thing is how the canes are creatively incorporated into the design.

"Treasure Box" by Dayle Doroshow. Doroshow presents her beautiful art on a polymer clay backdrop that is both functional and in complete unity with the design of the jewelry.

Cards by Deborah Anderson. These delightful cards feature polymer canes and impressions that can also be used as jewelry.

canes should be evenly sliced and placed with precision, and the surface should be even and smooth as intended in the design.

A beautiful bead is best displayed with quality components. Even the bead holes are a consideration in refining the quality of the bead design. When designing jewelry, the inclusive clasps, chains, jewelry findings, and beads all reflect on the artist's investment in quality. A cheap spacer or string can demerit an otherwise attractive work. Considering these expenses in the design will enable you to plan efficiently without compromising the quality. Clasps, hinges, pedestals, and hangings are an important function of the art and should be designed in unity with the entire piece.

If a frame is warranted, it should complement the art and simply not just "frame" the piece. Many artists have made their own frames and carriers as a display feature of the art. Even the box or bag the art is stored in is part of the complete presentation.

It may go without saying that you should always sign your work, but in polymer clay this also can be the opportunity for a creative component. Several artists have made signature canes or designed stamps to sign their work. Some include a signature bead or tag to credit the artist. When work is for sale, it should also be supplied with information regarding the care of the piece.

One of the most beneficial things an artist can do to increase the collected value of a piece is to photograph or document it properly. This is a tell-tale sign of the professionalism of an artist. The care an artist takes in this step is usually consistent with the care the artist delivers while designing the art. When presenting work to a gallery or a show, it is of crucial importance that the photography is of the highest quality. The photographs in this book are presented by talented, professional photographers who also consider their work in photography an art form. Their meticulous attention to detail is much appreciated by artists and viewers who can enjoy polymer clay art without having access to the actual work. The image of a beautiful piece of art can enrich the lives of many indefinitely.

Nancy Osbahr, Checkered Heart Studio. These pins are nicely finished with a signature cane. The clasp is held in place with a portion of clay.

Chapter 3

Materials and Supplies

All you really need to work in polymer clay is a few colors of clay, a work surface, a blade, an oven, and your hands; however, as you realize the unlimited potential of the medium, you may wish to create more variation in your designs. Using the correct materials will eliminate hours of frustration and prevent disappointment.

A good designer typically has the most beneficial tools, including ordinary items like a comfortable chair, good light, and hand wipes. Many common items from the kitchen and garden have appeared in studios as fundamental supplies, too. Organization of your tools will give you a head start on creativity, because an idea can be lost or abandoned while searching for a particular tool. Although it is a personal style of organization that each artist will develop, keeping the following items grouped together may help: clay, canes, varnishes and glues, sanding supplies, carving and shaping tools, blades and needles, pliers and wire snips, shape cutters, stamps, powders, foils, pencils and paints, findings, wire, and beads. Ordinary drawing tools such as tracing paper, pencils, rulers, a protractor, scissors, and a permanent marker (for signing) should

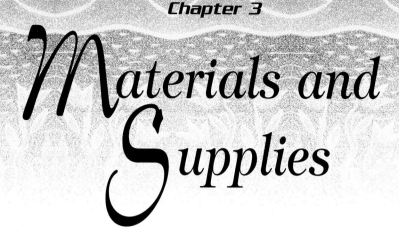

always be within reach. Also, don't forget to logically organize copier images, instructions, and articles with information regarding polymer clay.

The materials recommended here have won favor in the polymer clay community as a result of testing and comparing different manufacturers' brands of tools and supplies.

Polymer Clay

Polymer clays are most often distinguished by their manufacturer. This is true because different manufacturers incorporate different performance properties within their clays; therefore, all clays are not alike. I currently work with Accent Import-Export, Inc. (importers of Fimo clay), and my clay of choice is Fimo. All of the projects in Part 3 were created with Fimo clay because I am confident in the results achieved with Fimo. Obviously, when you are the creative director of a company, there is a bias toward appreciating products manufactured and distributed by that company; however, Fimo became my clay of choice independently, after experimentation with all of the brands and long before company affiliation. Nearly all of the manufactured brands of polymer clay are represented by use in the incredible art shown throughout the pages of this book. Choosing a clay is a personal choice based on design application, performance, and durability.

Popular polymer clays

Therefore, it is good to become familiar with the personality of each brand, not only to achieve desired applications, but also to avoid unwanted results. For example, certain clays may be adequate for making beads, but brittle when designing flat pieces. Further, an artist should be open to new clays and products, because formulations, colors, and performances are constantly being improved and developed by manufacturers. It is encouraged that artists communicate with manufacturers on the needs of the art community. Polymer clay has evolved as one of the most dynamic mediums of the century, and with active participation from both artists and manufacturers, it will continue to open the doors of creativity.

Polymer clay is found in most craft and art stores but is frequently purchased through mail order art suppliers because most stores do not carry all of the colors available, nor do they regularly carry special products such as liquid polymer. Most colors of polymer clay can be purchased in small blocks or large bricks.

Each brand of clay differs in chemical composition although they are all essentially PVC, polyvinyl chloride. A plasticizer keeps the material soft before the clay is cured. Polymer clay is rated non-toxic, as is verified by the seal on the package. It is recommended to accurately follow the baking and use instructions printed on packages, because they will vary slightly by manufacturer.

Translucency is another dimension of this manmade clay. Translucent clay can be tinted by adding tiny amounts of any color of opaque clay.

An oven thermometer is essential to assure accurate heating. Individual brands of clay will require slightly different baking temperatures.

A discerning artist will intentionally choose the desired translucency required in the total composition, whether it be incorporated as a surface technique or a theme of the piece. Different brands of clay will vary in opacity. Curing requirements may also alter the clay's opacity, and it is recommended to experiment with baking to reveal brand characteristics. The point is, these variations can increase options when designing a piece.

Popular Polymer Clays

CERNIT (T&F, GMBH): This clay is easily conditioned and has somewhat translucent qualities. Colors include primaries, glamour sparkle colors, and subtle heather tones. Cernit is strong and flexible and is particularly popular with doll makers because of its translucent quality in skin tones. Made in Germany and distributed by Kemper.

CREALL-THERM (HAVO B. V.): This is a good, soft clay. It is opaque and has good strength. Made in Holland, it is popular in Dutch schools.

FIMO MODELING MATERIAL (EBERHARD FABER, GMBH): Fimo Classic is intense, richly colored clay of excellent quality and strength. It is initially firm in conditioning and features popular art translucent and primary colors. Great caning properties and good image transfer quality and excellent endurance.

FIMO SOFT (EBERHARD FABER, GMBH): Fimo Soft is a dependable, strong clay when baked and is easy to condition. Strong, bright colors, fluorescent, glitter, stone, and translucent special effect colors.

FIMO PUPPEN (EBERHARD FABER, GMBH): This is a special doll-making formulation of Fimo clay.

GEMCOLOR (OMYACOLOR): This new clay is soft, pliable, and somewhat translucent. It offers graduated colors and pearls. Good strength. Made in France and not readily available in the U.S.

LIQUID SCULPEY (POLYFORM PRODUCTS, USA): Although it is not a solid, Liquid Sculpey is a polymer clay. It comes in opaque and clear formulations and is primarily used as a surface treatment or transfer medium.

Preparing clay and mixing colors with the help of a food processor

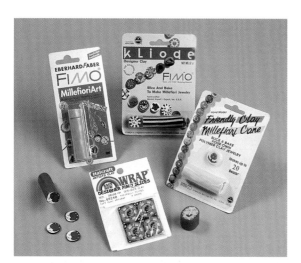

Examples of pre-made canes

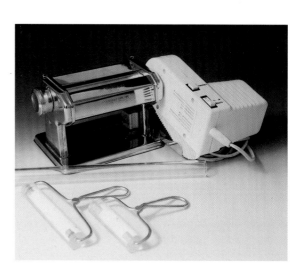

Lucite brayers and a pasta machine

PREMO (POLYFORM PRODUCTS, USA): Premo is easily conditioned and comes in brilliant painterly colors. The metallic colors have unique mica shifting properties. Premo, a recently developed formulation, replaces the Polyform clay Promat.

SCULPEY FLEX (POLYFORM PRODUCTS, USA): This special clay is formulated for elasticity after baking.

SUPER SCULPEY (POLYFORM PRODUCTS, USA): This is a very strong flesh-colored clay sold only in large blocks. It is often used as a base and covered with additional layers of clay.

SCULPEY III (POLYFORM PRODUCTS, USA): Sculpey III is very soft and easily conditioned. It comes in a full range of colors and is economic for use with groups.

Pre-made Canes

CLAYMATES (CROOKED RIVER, INC.): These canes are approximately 1" in diameter and sold in sets of three. Popular and seasonal motifs. Made of Fimo clay.

KALEIDOKANE DESIGNER CANES (ACCENT IMPORT): Designed by Barbara A. McGuire, Paulette Thiele, and Bryan Schaup, these canes are classic icon motifs of faces, flowers, stars, hearts, cats, etc. and are made of Fimo clay.

MILLEFIORI CANES (AMACO): These round and square canes are made of Friendly Clay and include quilt and floral patterns and translucent designs.

RAINBOW WRAP (HALLCRAFT, INC.): Incredibly intricately designed canes are sold already in slices, ready for use. Made with Fimo clay.

Clay Softeners

FIMO MIX QUICK (EBERHARD FABER, GMBH): This is a softening additive and clay extender made for Fimo clay.

SCULPEY DILUENT (POLYFORM PRODUCTS, USA): A few drops of Diluent are used as a softener or to aid in bonding baked clay pieces to raw clay.

Rollers and Pasta Machines

ROLL RIGHT LUCITE BRAYER: This handy acrylic brayer comes in 4" and 6" sizes.

DRINKING GLASS: A common drinking glass can serve as an excellent tool for flattening and smoothing clay.

ATLAS PASTA MACHINES: Atlas is the most recommended brand of pasta machine, noted for its quality and endurance. Some machines are equipped with attachments that cut clay into strips. A motor can be attached, which is very valuable for working with large quantities of clay. Manufactured in Italy.

TRATTORIA PASTA MACHINE MODEL # TBN200: This is a wide (nearly twice as wide as regular machines) front-loading pasta machine.

Wireform armatures for clay

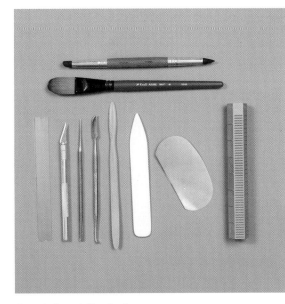

Assorted modeling tools

Blades and Mini-choppers

HANDI CHOPPER (BLACK & DECKER): This is a mini food processor that works well because the blade is attached to the shaft with a metal piece. Large-sized food processors are recommended to help condition large quantities of clay.

NUBLADE KATO (PRAIRIE CRAFT): This firm, 6" long blade was designed for polymer artists by Donna Kato.

NUFLEX KATO (PRAIRIE CRAFT): Also designed by Donna Kato, this blade is very flexible.

KEMPER (KEMPER ENTERPRISES, INC.): This large, ultra-thin piece of stainless steel can be used as a clean-up tool or for cutting when a blade is not appropriate.

THOMAS SURGICAL BLADES (THOMAS MEDICAL SUPPLY): These stainless steel blades are flexible and extremely sharp. Use with extreme caution.

X-ACTO KNIFE: This knife is a common graphic artists' tool available with a variety of interchangeable blade tips.

Armatures

WIREFORM MESH (PARAGONA): This woven mesh comes in various metals such as brass, copper, stainless steel, and aluminum. The many weaves accommodate different strengths. The aluminum is rustproof, lightweight, and serves as an excellent armature for large work.

Modeling Tools

CLAY SHAPERS (FORSLINE & STAR INTL. LTD.): These modeling tools have a rubber-like tip that is firm and comes in a variety of shapes such as points, flat chisel, and cup chisel.

DENTAL TOOLS: Stainless tools with varying fine tips useful for manipulating clay.

FEEL GOOD BONE FOLDER (SDK DISTRIBUTORS): Made of real bone, these classic straight-edge tools are popular for use in book-making crafts but are perfect for modeling and burnishing surface areas of polymer clay. They are available in rounded or pointed tips in 6" and 8" lengths.

FIMO CLAY TOOLS (EBERHARD FABER, GMBH): Handy shaping tools made of plastic. The set includes four double-ended tools in a pouch.

Carving and Piercing Tools

AWL: An awl is a traditional leather tool with a sharp tapered point. It is used for piercing holes in beads or pendants.

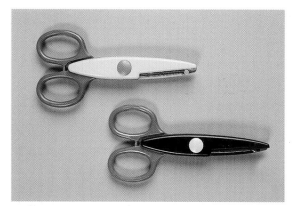

Craft scissors

Design cutters

DOCKYARD (DOCKYARD MODEL CO.): A high-quality brand of wood carving tools.

DOUBLE-ENDED DRILL TOOL (KEMPER ENTERPRISES, INC.): This useful tool features a wooden handle with two sizes of drills, one on either end. It is invaluable for making holes larger in beads that are already baked.

NEEDLES: A long needle secured to a wooden or metal handle is used for piercing beads.

SPEEDBALL LINOLEUM CUTTERS: These are traditional tools for carving block prints, available in several sizes. A special holder allows the artist to change cutters and replace them as needed.

Cut-out and Extrusion Tools

COOKIE CUTTERS: Ordinary cutters in various motifs are a common favorite to cut shapes.

FISKARS CRAFT SCISSORS (FISKARS INC.): Originally developed for memory album crafts, these scissors cut a variety of patterned edges.

FRIENDLY CUTTERS (AMACO): These tools are geometric shapes or those that correspond to leaves and petals.

KANE (KANE INDUSTRIES CORP.): Specialty-edge craft scissors intended for paper, but can also be used with baked or unbaked clay.

KEMPER CLAY GUN (KEMPER ENTERPRISES, INC.): This cartridge and plunger tool is great for extruding soft clays. The tool comes with twelve design templates to extrude the clay.

KEMPER CLAY PUNCHES (KEMPER ENTERPRISES, INC.): Ultra-thin, long punches are used for removing tiny square volumes of clay from solid masses of clay; simply put, the tool removes a square hole through the clay.

KEMPER PATTERN CUTTERS (KEMPER ENTERPRISES, INC.): These cut-out tools come with a plunger that pushes the clay out of the cutter. They are available in various shapes (like stars, hearts, and geometric shapes) and progressive sizes.

WAX FLORAL CUTTERS (STANISLAUS IMPORTS): These large-sized cutters create the shapes to make three-dimensional roses, orchids, and other floral-type forms.

Specialty Tools

FISKARS PAPER CRIMPER (FISKARS INC.): A tool that crimps clay as it is pulled though special rollers.

JASI SLICER (JUDITH SKINNER, INC.): A unique slicing blade and carrier that guides the blade along a guidepost as the artist slices cane. Ultra-thin and even thicknesses of clay slices are achieved with this tool.

MARXIT (PRAIRIE CRAFT): This measuring tool designed by Donna Kato is a six-sided cylinder with linear impressions. Each side features a raised set of lines that evenly marks the clay. It is very useful for measuring strips of clay, beads, or cane slices in equal proportions.

PRECISION ANGLE AND MEASURING TEMPLATES: Dianna Crick and Rebecca Preston designed this system for squaring quilt canes. The measuring template helps to measure accurate amounts of clay for designing and color mixing.

WAVY BLADE (INTRODUCED BY MARIE SEGAL): This is an extremely sharp 5" blade bent into waves. This blade will cut into several layers of a block of clay, revealing colors and creating patterns in a prepared stack of clay.

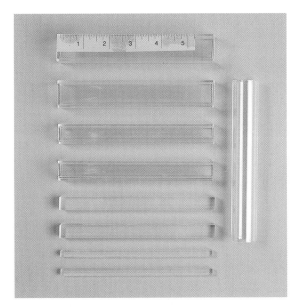

Quilt cane templates

Creative Clay Stamps

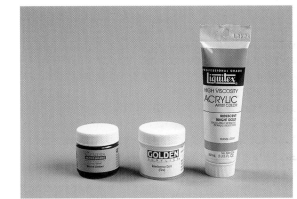

Polymer-friendly paints

Molds

DESIGN PUSH MOLDS (AMACO): Judi Maddigan has designed a variety of molds including bears, fruits, hearts, flowers, and angels.

JEWELRY FINDINGS: Brass stamped charms and findings can serve as molds.

WHAT A CHARACTER (AMACO): Known for her dolls and storytelling, designer Maureen Carlson has designed charming head, hands, and feet molds for polymer clay.

Rubber Stamps

AMERICAN ART STAMP: Original designs of American Art Stamp have bold, deep cuts that are perfect for use with polymer clay. Designs include big block patterns, Southwest themes, spirals, and classic styles.

COMMOTION, THE ART OF RUBBER STAMPING: Commotion has worked with several well-known artists to create exquisite stamps particularly to encourage the incorporation of stamped images into individual art. Signature design stamps feature elegant, current themes.

CREATIVE CLAY STAMPS (LIMITED EDITION RUBBER STAMPS): These double-sided positive/negative relief stamps are presented in Design Editions by Barbara A. McGuire and other polymer clay artists, for use especially with polymer clay.

READY STAMP COMPANY, SAN DIEGO: This non-profit organization will create a 6" x 6" sheet of rubber stamp material made from images you submit. The company supplies both the positive (the stamp) and negative (the matrix) of the image.

UPTOWN RUBBER STAMPS, INC.: Uptown's popular Running Rhino features whimsical designs with floral, heart, and nature motifs.

Paints

GENESIS POLYMER PAINTS (AMACO): Similar to traditional oil and acrylic paints, these newly developed paints are cured by heat setting.

GOLDEN ACRYLICS (GOLDEN ARTIST'S COLORS, INC.): Some formulations of these acrylic interference paints are made with a UV (ultraviolet) protectant.

LIQUITEX ARTISTS COLOR (BINNEY & SMITH): These opaque acrylic paints are particularly popular for "antiquing" simulated ivory or stone.

Colored pencils and markers

Examples of gold leaf

Pencils and Pens

Note: Some pens, although labeled permanent, may bleed into the clay after several years time. For that reason, many artists avoid pens altogether and use a signature cane or stamp to sign their work.

IDENTI PENS (SAKURA): These markers are dual-point permanent, waterproof, and acid-free colored inks.

PEN TOUCH CALLIGRAPHY METALLICS (SAKURA): Available in several sized tips, these gold and silver metallic inks are permanent, waterproof, and acid-free.

PRISMACOLOR (SANFORD): These quality pencils have fine, permanent pigments and soft, thick lead.

SHARPIE (SANFORD): This pen is often used to sign work, but it should be noted that the ink may bleed into the clay over time.

Metallic Foils

EASY METAL (EBERHARD FABER, GMBH): This composite metal leaf comes in gold, silver, and subtle shades of gold-green and gold-red.

GOLD LEAF: You can use real gold leaf to enhance your finest creations.

MAGIC LEAF (BLATTMETALL GMBH & CO. KG): Beautiful hand-burnished patterns of circles, stars, lines, and square blocks are available in gold or copper leaf. Magic Leaf composite leaf also comes in shades of sunset red and steel blue, as well as bulk packages of gold and silver.

METALLIC HEAT TRANSFER FOILS: Brilliant colors and holographic gold and silver transfer foil. These metallic foils are attached to a plastic release paper and set with heat.

Surface Alterations

CRAFTER'S PICK CRACKLING MEDIUMS (API ADHESIVE PRODUCTS, INC.): Crauqueleur finishes create fine or medium crackles for simulating aged surfaces. The crackles are made in a three-part process and may be defined in any color.

MODERN OPTIONS PATINAS (MODERN OPTIONS, INC.): These liquid chemicals will oxidize a metal base or metallic painted surface to create weathered metallic effects. Most finishes require a two-part process of undercoat and patina, although real metallic powder or ground metal flakes can also be used. The paints and patinas must be used with safety precautions. They also should be sealed to protect the final finish.

Patina

Crackling gel

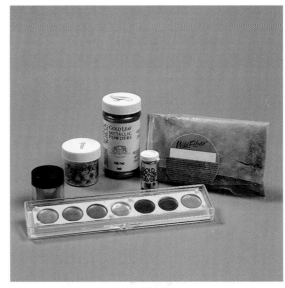

Powders and finishes

Mica Powders, Metallic Powders and Fibers, Chalks, and Glitters

DECORATING CHALKS (CRAF-T PRODUCTS, INC.): Available individually or in a convenient palette of twenty-five chalks, these chalks work well to softly color the surface of wet clay.

FIMO PULVER (EBERHARD FABER, GMBH): A true metal powder which results in beautiful metallic finishes. A dust mask is required and caution advised in regard to the metals.

GOLD LEAF METALLIC POWDERS (NEUBERG-EBEL): These high-quality metallic, mica, and pearl powders offer an incredible range of color. Sold in 2-ounce quantities.

JACQUARD PEARLESCENCE POWDERS (RUPERT, GIBONS, SPIDER): Popular because of the beautiful colors available and the non-toxic appeal of the mica from which they are made, Jaquard powders are sold in assortments and individual jars.

MINI METALLIC RUB ONS (CRAF-T PRODUCTS, INC.): Beautiful color assortments of metallic powders are held in a wax base. Packaged in a six-color strip.

PLASTIC CONFETTI AND GLITTERS by various manufacturers may be added to clay to simulate opals.

USARTQUEST MICA FLAKES (USARTQUEST, INC.): Real mica sheets and flakes are excellent for use with translucent clay to simulate stone, as well as provide surface interest.

WILDFIBER PAPER ADDITIVE (NEW BASICS): These special recipes of pre-mixed combinations of fiber-, glitter-, and paper-making materials can be applied on or mixed into polymer clay (especially translucent) to achieve special effects.

Finishes

ARMOR ALL PROTECTANT (ARMOR ALL PRODUCTS CORP.): Usually used for car upholstery, this liquid polish and cleaner can also be used to shine polymer clay.

FIMO VARNISH (EBERHARD FABER, GMBH): Available in both matte and gloss, water-based or lacquer, this varnish was especially formulated for Fimo clays. It is very strong and glossy.

SCULPEY GLAZE (POLYFORM PRODUCTS): This varnish was especially formulated for Polyform Products brand polymer clays.

Glues

E-6000 SILICATE GLUE (ECLECTIC PRODUCT, INC.): E-6000 will hold well initially but may deteriorate after four to five years of reaction with clay.

PVC PLUMBER'S GLUE: Available in plastic supply or home improvement stores, this glue was formu-

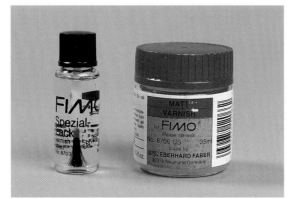

Varnish made specifically for polymer clay

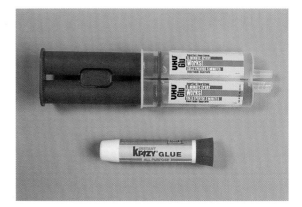

Adhesives

lated for gluing PVC plumbing pipes. It permanently adheres polymer to polymer.

SOBO GLUE (DELTA TECHNICAL COATINGS): This glue is used in the particular application of preparing surfaces before adhering polymer clay, including baked pieces of clay. It also works well when adhering paper to clay.

SUPER GLUE: A cyanoacrylate glue that bonds surfaces instantly.

TWO-PART EPOXY GLUE: Found in any hardware store, epoxy is a very strong, permanent, traditional jeweler's glue. Use in adequate ventilation.

ZAP A GAP: This cyanoacrylate glue is a thick formula which fills in small gaps between surfaces.

Wire

ARTISTIC WIRE (ARTISTIC WIRE LTD.): This high-quality colored copper wire comes in many colors and gauges. The wire can be fashioned into findings, as well as integrated into artwork.

COILING GIZMO (THE REFINER'S FIRE): An incredibly innovative machine, this "gizmo" wraps wire around a separate wire or rod. The resulting wire cord can be made into beads and findings.

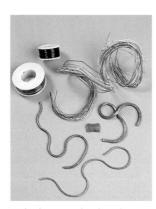

Telephone and colored wire

TELEPHONE WIRE: Common brightly-colored PVC-coated telephone wire is compatible for use with polymer clay

and may even be baked at low temperatures. Because the coating is very thin, tests should be run to confirm that the material can withstand the baking temperatures needed for curing polymer clay. You should also check with the original supply source (such as the telephone company) for additional cautions, for not all wires are made of the same materials.

WIG JIG: This is a great tool for bending wire into loops and curves to create clasps, hooks, and wire components.

WIRE WIZARD UNIVERSAL JIG: Designed by Corrine Gurry, this heavy metal jig allows artists to set pegs and tubes as templates for designing with wire.

Videos

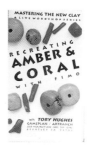

ABBA DABA PRODUCTIONS LLC (PRODUCED BY BETTE ABDU): These videos feature popular guest artists who share their individual tips and styles.

MASTERING THE NEW CLAY (GAMEPLAN ARTRANCH VIDEOS PRODUCED BY JEREMY GORDON): Polymer clay instructional videos are taught by Tory Hughes and other skilled artists. These high-quality videos cover nearly twenty different popular workshops, as well as basic design instruction.

MINDSTORM PRODUCTIONS: Several projects are included on each video that teach beginners, as well as accomplished artists, new techniques.

Technique videos

PART 2

Creativity

Concerning creativity, *there is the question of "Is creative ability innate, or is it learned?" I believe the answer is yes to both, because we are born with creativity and we learn how to use it. I am living proof of the latter in the fact that my own creativity has emerged profoundly as I have researched information to present in this book, even though I have been passionately involved in art all of my life. Hopefully the ability to deliver my creative expression has improved. The following two chapters reflect discussions with many of my friends, mentors, and peers. Most of them do not analyze their art in terms of the elements and principles reflected in their work— they have been educated in art and seem to apply these things subconsciously. This makes me believe that once you have learned to explore creativity and develop good design skills it then becomes a part of you. This book is meant to encourage your creativity, your continued learning, and a constant development and evaluation of your own design ability.*

Ultimately, an artist must utilize creativity and skill to serve the art. The strength of the piece must not rely on technique alone. Together, the potential of this incredible medium, and the creativity of an artist, awaken unlimited possibilities.

32

Chapter 4
Creativity and Design

Michael Grove

"Mysterious" by Michael Grove. Masks are always an intriguing expression of passion and creativity. Grove has continually approached polymer clay as a dynamic art medium, and his work reflects quality of design and the execution of expert craftsmanship.

Creativity is a natural thing. It is a contagious energy, a spark of discovery, curiosity, and learning by doing. Creativity is an innate purpose, a fulfillment, a physical manifestation of life. There are many outlets to creativity, including art, craft, song, dance, gardening, cooking, sewing, building, computer programming, and making an Internet website, to name a few. Creativity is doing. It is interesting to note one's attitude toward the things he or she creates. Does a person care for his or her creations and value, recall, keep, or give them away? Creativity is susceptible to our emotional nature and interaction with others: praise and approval, acknowledgment or indifference, dislike and rejection.

Terry Murphy

Karen Murphy. Sculptured forms communicate expressions of the human condition.

Mask by Donna Kato, author of
The Art of Polymer Clay. *The subtle
quality of the surface gives
emphasis to the character of the form.*

Vernon Ezell

Creativity is free. It costs nothing and has no limits. No one can own your creativity. It is of immense value, spiritually, and sometimes, monetarily. Creativity is vulnerable to judgment. What may be fashionable for one time may be passé for another. What may be a discovery for one individual may be "old hat" to another, for "What has been will be again, what has been done will be done again; there is nothing new under the sun" (Ecclesiastes 1:9). But, the priceless element in an act of creativity is that we are all individuals and therefore our creativity is unique to each of us. It is to your advantage to use your own personal creativity, because no one else has it, and to refine your personal creativity because it is a personal journey, a development of character, an act of discipline and the expression of hope in a result.

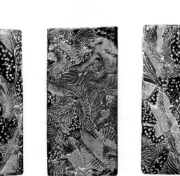

Freddi Lieberman

"Northern Lights" by Carol Steinman Zilliacus. This abstract composition is a reflection of the artist's vivid imagination and fearless exploration.

When approaching creativity, we can reflect on the uninhibited creations of a child, a child such as we once were. As adults, we need to eliminate restraints of fear, judgment, correctness, and social approval and embrace the freedom to create with innate confidence. Ralph M. Pearson puts it beautifully in a quote from *The New Art Education*: "Children are born creators and remain so until their native art impulses are killed by the imposition or imitation of adult standards concerned with skill and literal fact. For the young child, creation is a joyous adventure. It is a game using color or any medium as means to saying something in pictorial symbols with a happy recklessness which tosses skill and truth out the window without a quiver of hesitation or regret. It is automatically original because it flows with such bubbling freshness from within out. It is unself-conscious. There are no conflicts. A flash of vision melts into concept and concept into expression. Whatever that expression is is right. There is no wrong. From such divine self assurance divine creation must be born."

Creativity is always there. It is a sleeping giant. The creativity I address in this book is in reference to art. *Webster's Dictionary* describes art as "implying a personal, unanalyzable creative power," and design means **a:** to conceive and plan out in the mind and **b:** to create, fashion, execute, or construct according to plan.

Design is a plan. Through design, the energy of creativity is organized and transformed into a material substance, that substance being visual. Also, the ultimate end result is that something is seen by somebody. The art is communicated and interpreted. It is challenging to deliver the energy of creativity and expression into material substance, but initial choices help us direct our creative process and develop our design.

Composition is a word that describes the arrangement of elements in a design. When a design has been well-composed, the viewer has the ability to distinguish and compare the

"Power Rangers" by Timothy and Barbara A. McGuire. *This plate was created and traced from the drawings of a Timmy, five-year-old. The abstract line figures are Power Rangers, identified by their belts.*

Barbara A. McGuire

"Sometimes..." by Terry Lee Czechowski. This riveting and incredibly expressive piece is from Czechowski's "Life with Cancer" series. The composition clearly communicates the message of the artist.

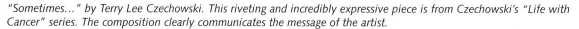

features in an arrangement. The composition helps the viewer to comprehend the theme or intention inherent in a design. If the composition is not obvious, the beholder is called upon to "complete" the ambiguous presentation, resulting in a variety of interpretations of the art.

Visual stimulation can be gratifying, calming, awe-inspiring, and a feast for the eyes. Yet, art can also be unsettling, intriguing, daring, or even disturbing. Visual stimulation arouses responsive feelings like happy, mad, sad, afraid, or embarrassed. Once we have established what we wish to express, we can utilize more definition, such as light, heavy, subtle, intense, playful, or serious, to get our point across. Then we can consider

sensual enhancements, including warm, cold, soft, hard, smooth, and rough, to add impact to our design. How about creating art that is exciting, relaxing, shocking, or funny? It is important that the design be reflective of choices that have something in common; the design should make sense. Otherwise, the piece will have a disoriented and unappealing character.

Ultimately with polymer clay, the personality and interests of the artist are creatively displayed, expressing one's nature. It is the embodiment of humor, sophistication, discipline, discovery, romance, satire, faith, tranquility, and taste. Polymer clay is like penmanship, a signature and a reflection of our life experiences. It is simply a

"Chaos Cards" by Dayle Doroshow. This incredible set of fractile designs is the theme to a game of inspiration. When the artist/player is stalled in a creation, revealing the cards will dictate a direction to pursue.

gift to enjoy this communication in dimensional and lasting form.

The design will have physical choices, two- or three-dimensional, stationary or mobile. It may be functional or simply expressive. Will you make a copy, a million copies (beads, for example), or just one? Decisions such as which audience you are appealing to, what cultural motifs may best serve your design, what time frame in history you are drawing from, or even the representational style such as abstract or formal will organize your expression before you begin to work.

We can take materials and techniques for granted. What really matters is you. You are the only person you have to satisfy with your creativity. Sometimes it is really hard to make a choice because we don't know what we want. We want to do it all. But, if you do one thing really well, you will master it and then you can move on to the next and the next.

Edwin C. Hansen III

"Chef Grape at Fast Eddie's" by Sheila Sinclair. Sinclair creates humor and delight in her poolside chef.

Ideas and Creative Freedom

The incredible sharing of knowledge and ideas has thrust polymer clay into art far beyond its humble beginnings as a modeling material. It is the desire of the polymer community to increase that flow of ideas and discoveries, enriching and bringing joy to the lives of many people. Ideas are an intensely personal experience. They are nurtured and born into reality through the investment of time and talent and plain hard work. It is of importance that the investment of an individual artist's efforts to develop an idea be treated with respect and gratitude. No one shares an idea in order to restrain another person from creativity. No one can lay claim to the spiral, seed bead, or alphabet. There is a great deal of synchronicity in discovery when a number of people are thinking similar thoughts. But, it is important that as artists we respect the opportunity for other artists to present their work in an environment where they are not competing against people with whom they have previously shared their knowledge. It is impossible to be in many places at once. In a world where ideas are so accessible, it is up to our own dignity not to compete with the development of a style of an artist merely because of a geographical or timely advantage.

"Meals on Wheels" by Donna Kato. Kato has generously written numerous magazine articles, making polymer clay an attractive medium to artists of all skill levels. Her design talents enable her to approach any number of applications of clay.

Vernon Ezell

George Post

Kathleen Dustin. Dustin's exquisite work has won acclaim as a fine craft. Her knowledge of the elements and principles of design allows her to develop any technique into a style of her own.

"Gylph Blade" by Nan Roche, author of The New Clay. Roche uses personal interests, as well as experience in other media, to develop new work in polymer clay.

Chris Roche

"Circle Pin" by Steven Ford and David Forlano. Known as City Zen Cane, Ford and Forlano have amazed the art community with their design quality and precision techniques. The complete value range of each color and use of geometric design has been a signature style.

Most frequently, when we are in a state of learning, we become excited, creative, and zealous to expand expression. Many people, including myself, have innocently tread forward when it is more appropriate to allow the originator of an idea or style to disclose and develop a particular theme. The solution to this occurrence is heartfelt self-scrutiny, restraint of ambition to capitalize on a creative idea, and open communication with peers. When you learn a new effect, style, or technique, return again to the basic elements and principles of design to express your own creativity incorporated with a learned technique. You will find there lies the opportunity to give more than to receive.

Ideas and Creative Freedom

Tory Hughes

George Post

Above: "Safe Travel Passes" by Tory Hughes. Hughes has completely embraced the richness of culture in art. She continually gives her energies in helping others to nurture their creative spirit.

Left: Martha Breen. Many artists such as Breen find spiritual reflections in their art, which is delivered with beauty and passion.

The nature of art is that beauty is in the eye of the beholder—there is no right or wrong. All art is subject to opinions, tastes, and preferences. The artists represented here have generously allowed their work to be published in order for others to enjoy their creativity as well as inspire others in their individual personal creativity. They are acknowledged for their willingness to share, their noted accomplishments, and their sheer passion towards their work, something that precedes all great art.

PART 3

Elements and Principles of Design

The study of any one of the elements or principles of art goes way beyond the presentation of these pages. Color alone merits in-depth study and practice throughout many years. The purpose of Part 3 is to familiarize persons who may not have a formal art education with general definitions and concepts. It is by no means a complete presentation of these terms, and further research is recommended. In some cases, certain information was intentionally omitted in order not to disclose an incomplete discussion or an "exception to the rule" type of application. Actual polymer clay artwork is used to illustrate the concepts in action rather than diagrams. After each topic, a project is presented to reinforce a concept of the element or principle presented. The projects are suggestive tools for learning, and individual variation is encouraged. The Glossary, Artist Directory, and Resources featured at the end of the book will assist you further in any information you may require.

Ralph Gabriner

Pin by Steven Ford and David Forlano of Citizen Cane. Notice the excellent use of all of the elements of design: line, space, texture, and rhythm.

This Part is arranged in chapters presenting first the elements of design, then the principles. Elements of design are: value, color, form, shape, line, space, and texture. These are the tools an artist uses to communicate. Each element has a character given to it by the artist. The elements do not stand independently but are integrated and joined to each other. For instance, a shape may have texture, and a line may have color. The artist that is aware of the impact of each of these elements will have the means to flourish in design. Principles of design are: balance, pattern, rhythm, movement, contrast, emphasis, and unity. These are the relationships between the elements, how the elements interact and respond to each other to make the design a whole. The principles of design dwell on the human nature of order, association, and differentiation of presented material; they reflect our established stability and acknowledgment of change. Composition is another word for the arrangement of the elements or the layout of the design.

Much of this material was referenced from a concentration of art instruction between the 1940s and 1960s—a dispersing of information emphasized during the Bauhaus period (1930s) in modern craft design. The basis for good craft was established as the three Cs: Composition, Creativity, and Craftsmanship. It was applied to nearly every field of study, including product design, architecture, graphic design, and fine craft. Today, our horizon is broadened by the tools, materials, and information we have at our disposal, but our reliance on creativity, workmanship, and the foundations of design elements and principles remains the same.

John Fago

"Black Spade Pelican" and "Black & White Heart" by Celie Fago. The clean, dynamic line, stark contrast, and elegant polished form complement the sleek design of the silver metal work. The art is completely unified in its presentation.

Chapter 6
Value and Color

Many design books begin with a discussion on value and color. This, perhaps, reflects the importance of choice of color in a design; understanding how color works and deciding what your preferences are can be a lifetime study. This chapter was written from a large amount of information supplied by Margaret Maggio and Lindly Haunani, two artists who have a passion for color and have educated many polymer clay artists. What this chapter intends to accomplish is to define color and value in descriptive terms so that your choices can reflect intelligent decisions as well as instincts. It will encourage you to discover colors you may not ordinarily use, so your work will be constantly fresh. The text presents information about the properties of value and color. Mixing color is not an element of design, but rather a process to achieve the color (the element) you have chosen for the design. There is no absolute language in defining color. Different authors will describe a concept or theory with similar, but perhaps not the same, terms. Concepts regarding color can be somewhat difficult to grasp, but if you understand the properties and personalities of colors, your instincts regarding color will be refined.

"Woven Illusions" by Laura Liska. The placement and change in value create movement and rhythm in these beads by Liska, who won the 1996 Embellishment Award for her design.

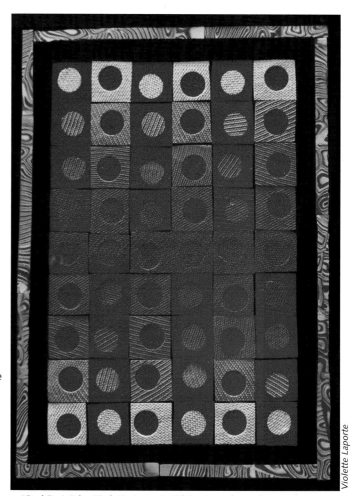

Violette Laporte

"Red Dots" by Violette Laporte. This piece shows how value helps us "see" texture and also how texture creates "perceived" value.

Value

Value refers to how light and dark each element is. The extremes are white and black, and the variations are anything in between. Light value is often called a high value, and dark value is often called a low value. These descriptions are relevant to context: a gray circle is light on a black background but is dark on a white page.

Value helps us understand form or volume of an object on a two-dimensional plane. In a portrait, the change in value of the skin tones helps to define the character of the face. In this case, the lighter values bring the plane forward, as in the nose and chin. Darker values describe the shadows or receding areas of the form. Dimensional quality can be created in design by varying the values of the shapes.

Texture can create value because of the way it reflects and absorbs light. Even though it may not be applied value, a surface that is not smooth will have shadows. The deeper the shadows, the more dramatic the definition, even though the value is merely a perceived experience. In this way, a design can employ value contrast simply by incorporating texture.

Changing the value can purposefully draw attention to an element or create movement. A color or element with graduating values can lead the eye because the progression from light to dark (or vice versa) is a familiar occurrence in nature. A sunrise or sunset is a good example of a natural progression in value. When an element differs greatly in value, the contrast will draw attention and create defini-tion. Contrast in value defines the type on this page. If the letters were gray, they would not be so easily seen.

Linda E. Merrill. Value contrast draws attention in these non-objective theme pins.

"Perfect Pin" by Dan Cormier. Cormier employs value to create depth in the geometric shapes in this incredible pin. The perfection of his craftsmanship also enhances the design.

George Post

Value can also support a design emotionally. Lightness refers to happy, carefree, arid, soft, and spring, whereas darkness refers to heavy, depressed, enclosed, and winter. Low contrast values can add peacefulness, calmness, and serenity to a design, and high contrast value can add sensation, impact, or excitement. Sometimes we choose a value subcon-sciously, but our design will have more impact if we remember that value is an element that we can purpose-fully utilize.

Steven Ford and David Forlano. The full range of value City Zen Cane employs in its colors gives the art a dimen-sional appearance.

Watch Your Step

This project illustrates how a shape can jump forward or recede according to the assigned value. Value is used by some artists to create optical illusions. The placement of value also helps us organize the design and make sense of the composition. If one section were out of sequence, the design would be confusing.

Materials

3 different colors of clay (1 light, 1 mid-range, and 1 low value)
Tracing paper, pencil, roller, blade, pasta machine
Optional: card stock, Sobo Glue

1. Condition the clay.

2. Use Fig. 1 to create a geometric set of shapes that implies an optical illusion. (See Fig. 3 for an additional option not shown in the photograph.)

Fig.1

3. Cut out small paper patterns of these simple shapes (Fig. 2). (Choose any piece of the design for Fig. 3.)

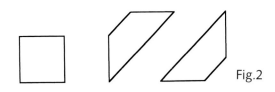

Fig.2

4. Roll the clay flat, about 1/16" thick, and cut out the different shapes responding to the appropriate colors; the photo is only a suggestion. You may assign the colors as you wish, as long as they are consistent with the dimension implied in the design.

5. Bake the pieces.

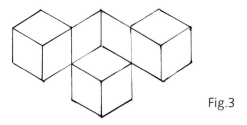

6. Randomly play with the value and dimension the value creates by placing the colors in different spots on the original drawing. Fig. 3 consists of one shape so it is easy to play around with the placement of value.

Fig.3

7. When you have an assemblage you like, you can glue it onto a sheet of card stock paper with Sobo Glue. This creates a background for your exercise.

*R*ing Around the Value

This is an exercise that illustrates how tints (additions of white) and shades (additions of black) of color result in lightening or darkening the value of a color. The exercise also illustrates how value changes lead the eye. A cookie cutter in a small people shape was used, but any shape will do (the amount of clay needed depends on the size of the cookie cutter). For accurate records of mixing, a pasta machine would be necessary but the same concept regarding value can be illustrated with proportions (in color mixing) that are not exact.

Materials

2 blocks medium-value clay (Fimo gold is shown)
1 block white
1 block black
Small people-shaped cookie cutter
Thin wire, roller, needle tool, pasta machine

1. Condition and roll out the blocks of clay into flat sheets, approximately 1/16" thick.

2. Cut out eight people of gold, seven of white, and two of black. Set one gold person aside.

3. Combine two gold with two white people; mix thoroughly. Roll out into a sheet. Cut out a person and set aside (Fig. 1).

4. Combine the scrap with another white person. Mix and flatten into a sheet. Cut out a person and set aside.

5. Continue the directions as described in Step 4 with the remaining white people (Fig. 2).

6. Combine two gold and the two black people; mix thoroughly. Roll out into a sheet (setting 1). Cut out a person and set aside. (You are now going to add gold to this combination, so you are progressing from equal proportions of gold and black to a mix that has more gold and less black. To keep adding black would make the ring very unappealing.)

7. Combine the scrap with another gold person. Mix and flatten into a sheet. Cut out a person and set aside (Fig. 3).

8. Continue with the directions described in Step 7 with the remaining gold people.

9. When all of the pieces are cut out, you should have: one white, one gold, five tints of gold (white with gold), and five shades of gold (black with gold). Poke tiny holes in the hands with a needle tool.

10. Bake all of the pieces.

11. When cool, arrange in value graduations and string through the holes with thin wire. Stand them up or spread them out in a ring (Fig. 4)!

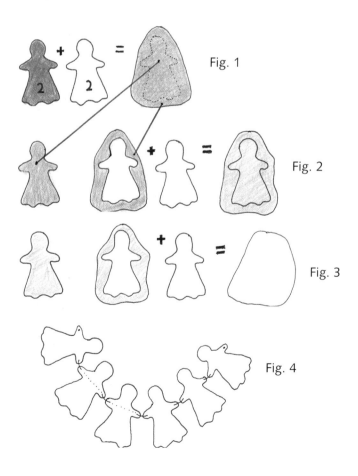

Fig. 1

Fig. 2

Fig. 3

Fig. 4

 olor

Roger Schreiber

"Fable Vessel" by Margaret Maggio. This splendid vase was created especially for the Master's Invitational Polymer Clay Exhibition & Sale in 1997 and illustrates a muted color palette.

Communicating with Color

Color is one of the most powerful design elements because it is evocative. This means that you can use colors to suggest just about anything: moods, feelings, a period in history or a certain style, a connection to nature or technology, or simply your personal preferences. The possible associations are limited only by your imagination and cultural conventions.

Try to take advantage of color's communicative abilities when choosing colors for a piece. Think about what you want the colors to say and select colors you believe are consistent with this message. There are no rules, for color is very subjective. What a color says to you may not be what it says to everyone, but that's okay—trust your instincts.

Color Properties

What a color is "saying" or how a color "feels" is related to the three properties of color: hue, value, and saturation.

Hue

We divide light into six spectrum colors (think about a rainbow). Hues are the "family names" we give to each of these spectrum colors. The names represent groups of similar hues and not single pure hues. The six hue families are: reds, oranges, yellows, greens, blues, and violets.

Hue Circles
(commonly known as a color wheel)

The six hues flow from one to the next in a continuum. It is impossible to show all of the steps from one hue to the next, so this continuum is usually diagrammed by a color wheel or, more accurately, a hue circle. See page 53 to create a color wheel.

Undertones

There is no such thing as a truly pure hue in any medium because every color has an undertone. Each of the six families can be split into two variations depending upon undertones. A green with a blue undertone is different from a green with a yellow undertone. You can easily place a color into one of these twelve hue zones by first determining which of the six hue families it falls into and then determining its undertone.

The previous section discussed value as an element in and of itself and how value relates to the other elements and the composition of the design. The following information speaks of value as a property of color.

The reason we see color is because objects reflect and absorb light. Value refers to how much light is reflected by the color. A value scale (or gray scale) is used to diagram value. If the eye is not trained, a good way to determine value in color selections is to take a photocopy (the gray scale) of the colors. The possible range is infinite, but on an ordinary value scale, anywhere from five to ten steps are usually shown between black and white. Here is a sample scale with five value zones:

White (Highest Value)

5	Light Grays	Pale Yellows/Creams
4	Medium-Light Grays	Yellows
3	Medium Grays	Oranges
2	Medium-Dark Grays	Red/Greens
1	Dark Grays	Blues/Violets

Black (Lowest Value)

Note that the six spectrum colors are not all the same value. ("Pure" violet is much closer in value to black and "pure" yellow much closer to white.)

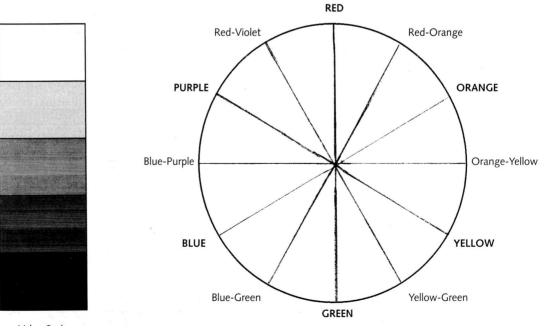

Value Scale

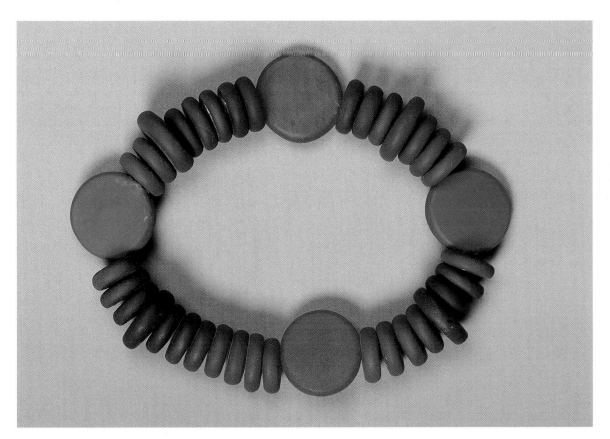

Double primary bracelet by Margaret Maggio. This study, which mixes two versions of "red" and two versions of "blue," illustrates how the colors can differ in undertones.

A value shift toward white is called a **tint**. Pinks are tints of red.

A value shift toward black is called a **shade**. Navy is a shade of blue.

When designing Millefiori canes, your value contrasts can become even more important than hue contrasts, especially if you plan to reduce the cane. Imagine a green face. As long as there are three darker valued areas that read as the eyes and the mouth, the image will read as a face regardless of the colors used.

Saturation

Saturation (or intensity) describes how pure a color is compared to the purest possible version of the color. There are infinite degrees of satura-

Color gradation by Dotty Calabrese. The tints and tones in this jewelry set create contrast in value. Notice the effect of black in the composition.

George Post

tion, but it's easiest to imagine just four distinct zones of saturation:

1 "Pure": As close to the spectrum version as possible
2 Muted: Still identifiable as one of the six hues but toned down
3 Desaturated: Not easily identifiable as one of the six hues (earth tones)
4 Neutral: Variations of blacks, grays, and whites

Designing a Palette

When planning a project or piece, try to visualize your finished product before selecting the range of colors, or palette.

Imagine saturations first:
Will most of the colors be pure/muted/desaturated/neutral?

Right: "Balloons" by Pier Voulkos. By mixing translucent clay with bright intense colors, Voulkos achieves a change in value that enhances the dimension in her dynamic forms.

Below: "In the Wind" by Judith Skinner. The desaturated color in the necklace is wonderfully reminiscent of fall. The same composition in another color would present a completely different feeling.

Vince Riggio

How will you be using neutrals/metallics?

Imagine values second:
Do you want to tint all of the colors? (Pastels)
Do you want to shade all of the colors?
(Deep/rich)
How much value contrast do you want/need?

Imagine hues last:
How many hues do you want?
Do you want the hues to be similar or different?
What undertones will each of the hues have?

Combining Colors

Once you have selected all of your colors, there are still some important factors you need to consider before putting them together in a project:

Simultaneity (or Simultaneous Contrast): The appearance of colors will change depending on what colors are next to them or surround them. Because it is difficult to predict these changes, the best thing to do is run a few tests. (Refer to the contrast project, page 124.)

Visual weight: Colors have different visual "weights." This means impact or attention, usually having to do with the balance of the composition. A small amount of intense color may have a large amount of visual weight.

Proportions: Once you have selected all of your colors, you may want to consider their relative proportions in the project. What color(s) will be dominate? What colors will be accents? What colors will you use as background or outline?

Above: "Flower Box" by Virginia V. Sperry. The saturated colors in this box are intense and vibrant.

Right: "Folk Beads" by Margaret Maggio. The yellow hue in these beads has a different appearance depending upon the adjacent color, illustrating simultaneous contrast.

George Post

"Red Teapot" by Rebecca Zimmerman. Zimmerman won an award for color at the 1998 Arrowmont Conference—Making History. The art is now a part of the Accent Import museum and illustrates excellent presentation of a dominant color.

Mixing Colors: Mixing colors in polymer clay is just like mixing colors in paint, except that it is much easier to measure solid proportions (as in polymer clay) than paint. The clay is simply measured and blended. Always record your work to enable you to duplicate a color later.

FRACTIONAL PROPORTIONS FOR COLOR MIXING

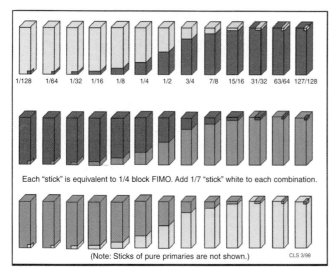

1/128 1/64 1/32 1/16 1/8 1/4 1/2 3/4 7/8 15/16 31/32 63/64 127/128

Each "stick" is equivalent to 1/4 block FIMO. Add 1/7 "stick" white to each combination.

(Note: Sticks of pure primaries are not shown.) CLS 3/98

George Post

Swap Group Primary Color Strands. This color study of Fimo primaries was an Internet swap hosted by Carol L. Simmons. The beads' strands serve as reference to exact color mixing, as shown in the chart at left, designed by Simmons.

Polymer Clay Color Wheel

This exercise in mixing color extends the traditional "primary" and "secondary" wheel to include an entire range of color by means of a "Skinner Blend" technique. Judith Skinner has discovered and shared this technique which easily enables graduated color blends of any number of colors. In this exercise we will blend two colors at a time. You will need any red, yellow, and blue. Every color of clay will differ in its character: some colors may be more transparent than others, some may have a more concentrated pigment or tinctoral power, and some may have undertones that distinguish the hue, such as a lemon or golden yellow. These variables will affect the color mixes. It is recommended to consistently record your findings for future use; your work will be more unique as you invent your own colors.

Materials

1 block red clay*
1 block yellow clay*
1 block blue clay*
Pasta machine, blade, mat board or card stock, tracing paper, protractor, pencil, scissors, Sobo Glue, permanent marker

*Red, yellow, and blue are the three primary colors. They are called primary because you can not achieve them by mixing any other colors.

1. Condition a sheet of each clay color (reserving some for Step 8). Cut each sheet into two long right triangles, each the same size.

2. Place the primaries adjacent to each other as shown (Fig. 1). You will have three sets of triangles: red/yellow, red/blue, and yellow/blue.

3. Fold the sheets, overlapping the colors as shown (Fig. 2).

4. Run it through the pasta machine.

Fig. 1

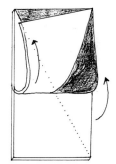

Fig. 2

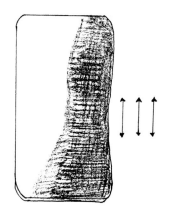

Fig. 3

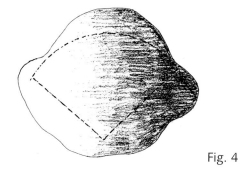

Fig. 4

5. Fold it again in the same direction. Be careful not to switch directions or you will completely blend the colors (Fig. 3).

6. Bake the three sheets.

7. Cut the pieces into wedges (100° angle) to create each portion of the color wheel as shown (Fig. 4).

8. Cut thinner wedges (20° angle) of each packaged primary (red, yellow, and blue).

9. Assemble the wedges on a mat board or card stock to illustrate the color wheel (see photo). Glue in place with Sobo Glue.

In this example, you blended three sheets: red to yellow, yellow to blue, and blue to red. The middles of these sheets produced secondary colors: orange, green, and purple. These secondaries are the combination of two primaries.

When you add all three primaries in equal proportions, you get mud. The mud will vary, however, from the undertones and amounts of the primaries. Mud is a tertiary color, although not all tertiary colors are mud. Tertiary colors indicate the presence of all three primaries. The resulting color depends greatly on the amounts of each primary (and the undertones in the primary). To illustrate this we will mix the color complements in a Skinner Blend.

In the next part of this exercise, each primary is pared with its complement, which is the secondary color across from it on the wheel.
Red with green (a combination of one half blue and one half yellow)
Yellow with purple (a combination of one half red and one half blue)
Blue with orange (a combination of one half red and one half yellow)

The mid portions will result in slates, russets, and olives, which are tertiary colors.

Materials

1/2 block red, yellow, and blue clay
1/2 block portion of orange, green, and purple clay
(mixed from the previous primaries)
Pasta machine, blade, permanent marker

1. Condition the clay.

2. Mix the orange (a combination of one half red and one half yellow), purple (a combination of one half red and one half blue), and green (a combination of one half blue and one half yellow).

3. Roll each color into a flat sheet and cut out long right triangles of each color. Place the primaries and secondaries adjacent to each other as shown above at right: red with green; yellow with purple; blue with orange.

4. Blend the colors using the same procedure (the Skinner Blend) as directed in the color wheel (page 53).

5. Trim the sheets into rectangles, the primary progressively blending to the secondary (Fig. 1 and shown above at left).

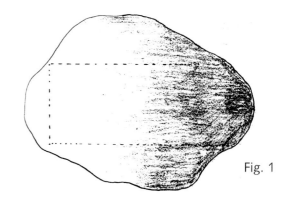

Fig. 1

6. Bake the sheets.

7. Label the color recipe (using the assigned manufacturer's color numbers, including secondaries) for future reference with a permanent marker.

Chapter 7
Form and Shape

Above: Joanne Bañuelos. Bañuelos uses sleek, stylish, organic form in her delightful sculpture.

Right: "Fall Beads" by Pier Voulkos. These amazing flat beads dance with the subtle reflection of the mica shift in the clay. The form is interesting yet allows the surface design to be the focus of the work.

The words form and shape are synonyms. They are used to describe the appearance of an object apart from the material itself. They are often used with adjectives such as a beautiful form or a square shape. Many times a person will use the word "shape" to describe something that has form. A "flower" shape is rendered in two dimensions, such as in a drawing or painting. The flower itself has form, a three-dimensional character of the flower. In this chapter, we will look at the qualities and characteristics of shape and form, what they communicate, and how they interact with the other elements and principles.

George Post

Form

Forms are three-dimensional. They contain volume, mass, and physical space. Form has height, width, and depth and can be geometric, as in squares and triangles, or organic, as in fruit and the human form. Abstraction of forms means to simplify the dimensional rendition to the basic nature of the object. Forms that do not represent anything at all are called non-objective. Realistic forms portray things as they actually are. It is common for forms to contain space, as in architecture. Forms can also surround without totally enclosing space, as in the case of a bowl. They can be thin, thick, or made entirely of a network of related mass. Forms do not have to be big, solid, or stationary. Raindrops are forms that change and move.

In design, it is advantageous for the form to serve the design's purpose. For instance, it would not be wise to design a form for a vase that is top-heavy, nor would it to design a box you could not reach into. A mask can still cover a face and have many different forms, but a mask still needs eyes or the wearer cannot see. However, form can be appreciated solely for the sake of form.

Additional considerations of form are technical quality and surface area. Craftsmanship affects form, like corners that do not match or surfaces that are not intended. Indeed, it is the surface area that is going to reflect light and thereby draw visual emphasis to the form. When working with polymer clay it is particularly important because very smooth, even surface areas require skill to achieve. Texture, simulated texture, or design images can lessen the attention to imperfections of the surface but cannot compensate for poor execu-

Jody Bishel

"Thistle Jar" by Jody Bishel. The incredible organic form in this vessel is designed to have stability.

tion of the surface. It is best to consider the surface finish early in the design plan.

Forms can be altered, developed, and enhanced by the addition of forms. Forms can be built on or expanded into complete forms; for example, add legs to a bowl or a top to a box, and two forms become one. Many forms are a combination of separate units. When these forms have styles in common, a unity or continuity is achieved.

Another way to alter a form is to break the surface. This can be done with an indentation or hole or by carving out a mass, which is essentially subtraction from the form to create an alternate form. These variations, addition and subtraction, in the form's surface area will attract attention. The same rule applies as in the other elements.

"Fertility Goddess" by Carolyn Potter. This human form rendered from translucent clay utilizes a smooth, shiny surface to enhance the design.
Michael Leonard

Right: "Book Box" by Cynthia Toops; lampwork glass by Dan Adams. Made of polymer clay and enameled glass, this form uses the successful combination of many forms to balance the composition.

Above: A. Ping Yeh. Yeh breaks the surface of the form to add interest and spatial depth to her stylish design.

Roger Schreiber

Unnecessary forms should not be included in the design, like a fifth wheel.

A form's effectiveness is particularly sensitive to context; because it embodies a volume and relies heavily on balance. This can be explained by the shape of earrings. A complementary shape of an earring will balance the shape of the head. All heads are different and that's why different earring forms look better or worse on different people. Another good example is a bead pendant. The form carries a weightiness that must be compensated for in the balance of the design of the rest of the necklace. The form is in or out of balance relative to its context.

The goal is to make an interesting form or a form that does not compete with, but complements, an interesting focus. In no other medium is there such spontaneous discovery of form than polymer clay—it is completely responsive. It also should be considered an advantage that complete individual forms can comprise the texture for a surface area. This is commonly found in nature as tendrils, leaves, and cones, and can be mimicked in polymer clay.

How does one achieve a form? Considering clay is somewhat soft for the construction of weighty masses, an armature is generally incorporated into the design. This can be seen as a limitation, but also as an opportunity for creativity. Tin foil can help to structure a solid form, and wire form mesh can add strength to a vertical form that is not an enclosed mass. More obviously, a ready-made form can be employed; a teapot is a container with the added personality of a handle and spout.

Simple shapes can become complex or interesting when they are protruding or stacked, having depth and dimension. Forms can interlock, as in a chain. All in all, the form is going to be the format for the design. It will become the surface area on which the image is placed, the texture is applied, and the creativity is expressed.

"Wearable Vessel" by Gwen Gibson. The simplicity of the pattern enhances this sleek, elegant form.

Robert Diamonte

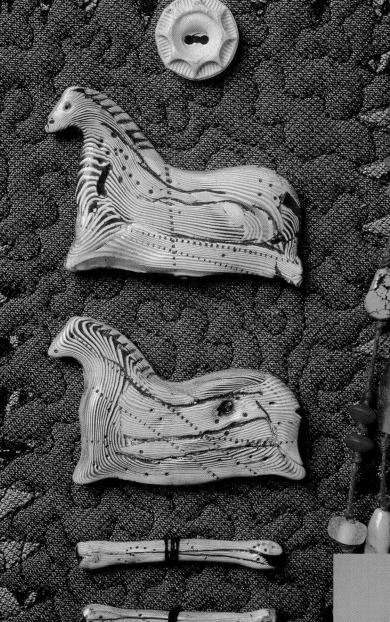

Jeff Baird

*Above: "Horse Shrine Lascaux Series 1998" by Luann Udell. Her
subtle use of form applied to the surface of her art richly enhances
her beautiful wall quilts. This was the winner of 1998
Embellishment Small Wonders Competition.*

*Right: "Crayon Beads" by Lindly Haunani. This playful translucent
bracelet illustrates imaginative form. The individual forms work
together as a whole to create rhythm and movement in the design.*

Mr. Potato Form

This exercise suggests creating all sizes of different forms, both organic and geometric, to playfully decorate and randomly attach to a main "body," which is a textured "form." The idea is to experiment with color and the surface design; notice how they both can complement or dominate the attention given to the form.

Materials

Assorted colors (your choice) of clay
4 oz. scrap clay*
3 to 6 ft. aluminum foil
1 ft. of 1/16" diameter wood skewer, cut into 1"
sections
Card stock, Sobo Glue, roller, blade, needle tool,
cornstarch, texture (your choice), pasta machine

*Scrap clay is any "discard clay"; for example,
distorted cane ends, trimmed edges, etc.

1. Create a form out of "crunched" tin foil. Once you have made a form you like, smooth the outside by rubbing it on a flat work surface, such as a sheet of card stock.

2. Cover the entire surface of the form with scrap clay. You can use newly conditioned clay if you wish, but using scrap clay may be more economical. Smooth the clay surface. Poke a 1/16" skewer piece into several places in the surface, creating holes. This will be where you stick the decorations into the Mr. Potato Form (Fig.1).

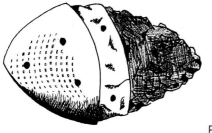

Fig.1

3. Bake the form. When it is cool, coat it with Sobo Glue, let it dry, and cover the entire form with a thin layer (sheet) of solid clay. Apply a surface texture by coating the clay with cornstarch and pressing in texture. In this example, Lego building bricks were used. Reopen the holes on the surface with the dowel and bake.

4. Now make the extensions. They should be lively colors, complementary to the base. Using black and white will make your piece more whimsical and help the colors to harmonize. Create small forms such as half circles, spiral shells, zigzags, elbows, eyes, snakes, lollipops, etc. They can have dots, stripes, or texture, but keep it very clean and simple. To add a completed finishing touch, "cap" the ends of the extension forms with a small disk of clay where they are intended to meet the body. Embed the 1" lengths of cut 1/16" skewers into the forms. It may help to drill a preliminary hole into the extension forms with a large needle tool in preparation of accepting the dowel. (See instructions for drilling bead holes on page 12.) (Fig. 2)

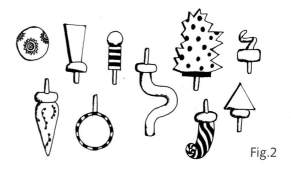

Fig.2

5. (Optional; not shown) Create a few larger "feet" forms on which Mr. Potato Form can stand. These can be cones, cubes, half circles, pyramids, etc. They should have a broad, flat base.

6. Bake the extensions with the dowels intact. If they are loose after baking you can always glue them in place with Sobo Glue.

7. Create your sculpture by attaching the extensions. You can play around with the arrangements to create different presentations of your art.

Change a Form

In this project, we will analyze the inherent quality of an existing form and change its personality by adding additional forms. Use your imagination to add handles, a top, or a base. You could also "drape" clay onto a form to make a dramatic change in appearance.

Materials

Glass jar
Any color clay (Fimo soft white is shown)
Pencil, paper, blade, roller, pasta machine, cornstarch

1. Choose a bottle or jar that has an interesting form. Draw a few sketches of how you could change this form.

2. Cover the entire surface of the form by piecing thin, flat sheets (setting 4) of clay together on the form's surface. Try to eliminate any air bubbles by slicing into them at an angle, releasing the air. Smooth the seams (Fig. 1). When handling the form it may be helpful to wear thin latex gloves or coat the form with a light dusting of cornstarch. Handle the form delicately.

Fig.1

3. Next, create and attach the additional forms. The original form shown was changed by adding handles and a rim. The handles were made by cutting a long cylinder carefully in half and placing the halves on the sides of the form (Fig. 2). The rim was made by attaching a half cylinder to the existing rim and

Fig. 2

then shaving the curve off at an angle. Be sure to work carefully when you are using sharp blades to shave the clay (Fig. 3).

4. Bake the form. Now you can decorate the surface with additional clay, canes, carvings, colored pencils, markers, or by sanding and buffing. The form shown is still a work in progress!

Fig. 3

$\mathcal{S}$hape

Dixon Withers–Julian

Above: "Rainforest" by Diane Dunville. Beautiful leaf shapes enhance this lamp. The shaded color gives the design depth and variety.

Right: Kazuyo Kono. The shape used in these pins are of classic Japanese heritage. They reflect a culture that has an appreciation for simplicity, balance, and order.

Shape can be described as an area being two-dimensional and having height and width. Shapes can be defined with a line or filled with a solid or texture, implying a plane or mass. They can be geometrical or organic, as in nature. Abstraction is the reduction of shapes to their simplest form. Shapes are effective because they draw the eye to an area through recognition of the outline or implied image of a familiar object. The eye is drawn to the content and size of the shape (particularly when large) or the color of the shape. Shape can also be invisible and simply implied by the grouping of objects together, for example, a text block in the shape of a circle. Shape is used to define, draw interest, separate, and organize.

We also see shapes in context. If one shape is placed over another, spatial depth can be suggested. If shapes are duplicated, repetition can evolve into a pattern. Shapes can gain interest through contrast; for example, if a circle is presented in the company of many squares, the contrast will draw attention. When a line gains enough width it becomes a shape, and the ends of the line are more relative as properties of the shape. Horizontal shapes, or those with a flat bottom, give a sense of stability. Vertical shapes give a sense of height or upward mobility. Flowing shapes surrounded by space give a sense of flotation. Pointed shapes look sharp, and curved shapes appear smooth and soft. Shapes can also be used to lead the eye, especially in the use of shapes diminishing in size. A simple circle can appear stationary, but if it is connected to a helix, it gives the illusion of movement.

Shapes can also be related to positive and negative. They are either the object or the background. This can switch depending upon the focus. Shapes do not have to be outlined; they can be perceived as changes in value. For example, the rays of the sun have more i n d i v i d u a l strength as shapes if they are not all one color and value; they are seen independently.

George Post

"Sparky Bead" by Debbie Krueger. The shapes in this pendant come alive because they contrast with the color of the background. They also are surrounded by enough space to individually gain attention.

It is important to understand shapes because they are the building blocks of images. The body is composed of many shapes; for example, the features of the face can be broken down into shapes. It is a challenge in drawing to render the shape we actually see, not the shape we think we see; for example, is a tree really symmetrical or is it just balanced? Its branches are indeed not mirror images emerging from a vertical line, but a combination of many shapes together. Variety in shape can be more interesting to your composition. Be sure your shape is serving the intended purpose.

Shapes can be very comforting, as in the familiar shape of a heart, and they can be riveting, as in the shape of a lightening bolt. Our eye is not only attracted by a shape but it is presented with an interpretation. The eye wants to solve the unknown so it searches for the context to explain the shape.

Letters are a beautiful combination of shapes. Fonts are identified by the shapes in the letters. The personality of the font reflects the personality of the shapes.

Bill Bachuber

Margaret Maggio. Maggio exquisitely uses shapes of color in her series of watercolor pins.

Left: "Cricket Pin" by Margaret Regan. This elegant shape silhouetted against a contrasting background is dynamic enough to carry the entire piece.

Below: Amelia Helm. Shape communicates the theme of the images in Helm's classically beautiful mosaic work.

George Post

Jennifer S. Herzberg

Chapter 7

Shape Mobile

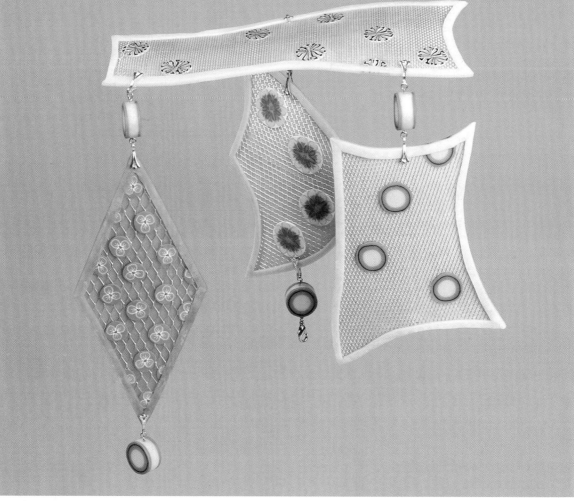

This project is called a shape mobile because its pieces, which are actually flat forms, can be described as shapes: a triangle shape, a star shape, a curvy rectangle shape, and an organic shape. The canes are also described as shapes: a circle shape or a triangle shape. The pieces in the mobile are reinforced with an embedded wire mesh and actually could be bent or bowed if desired. If you use translucent clay, the mobile will be illuminated when hung.

Materials

Four different colors of tinted translucent clay* (amount depends upon size of project)
1/2 block of three different colors of clay (choose colors that contrast, but won't clash)
Assorted canes (may be purchased pre-made, pre-made by you, or make additional bull's eye canes of different colors)
1-1/2 square ft. WireForm mesh, assorted weaves (as shown) if desired (weave size will not matter in this exercise)
Ten bails, six eye pins, jump rings
Fishing line or chain
Blade, brayer, needle-nose pliers, needle tool, pasta machine

*See general directions on tinting translucent clay

1. Condition (setting 3) and roll four thin sheets of clay, one from each of the translucent clays.

2. Cut out four random shapes out from wire mesh with a scissors. The mesh will give structure to the flat shapes and texture to the surfaces of the hanging pieces. The example shown used several weaves and different metals, giving variety to the piece. Place one mesh piece on each clay sheet (Fig. 1). Roll lightly with the brayer, not immersing, only securing the mesh onto the clay.

Fig. 1

3. Cut several thin, even strips about a quarter of the width of the flat clay (the color corresponding to the sheet) to finish the edges (Fig. 2). Lay this clay over the edges of the mesh shapes (Fig. 3). Using an X-Acto knife, recut the shapes out of the flat sheets.

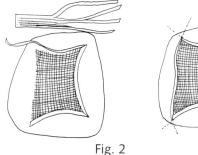

Fig. 2   Fig. 3

4. You can make canes to decorate and completely secure the mesh, or you can use pre-made canes for this project. To make a bull's eye cane, roll a cylinder of conditioned clay. Prepare a sheet of clay (approximately 1/8" thick) large enough to wrap around the cylinder. Trim the edges to create a straight guide line and wrap the cylinder with the sheet of clay. Trim the clay where it begins to overlap. The most important thing to remember

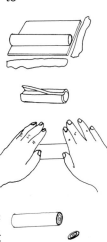

Fig. 4

about wrapping clay is that the edges should meet exactly, so there is a consistent thickness and therefore a consistent series of "rings" (Fig. 4). Continue with another layer of clay to make a cane with a core and two rings. This is a round cane and the shape of its slices will be round. A square cane is made by pinching or flattening the sides on the inside cylinder into a square form, and then successively wrapping each layer around that "squarish" form. A triangle cane is made by pinching the round cane down on a flat surface, creating a "tent" shape. Rotate the canes often to get even pressure as you shape the clay canes. The exactness of the canes will be more consistent with practice.

5. Decorate the surface of the mobile pieces with the cane slices by pressing them into the surface. The applied canes add surface interest and break the monotony of the large areas. This also helps to secure the mesh to the clay (Fig. 5).

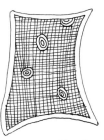

Fig. 5

6. Make spacer beads for the mobile by rolling a cylinder of solid color clay, slicing lengths 1/4" thick and placing a thinly sliced bull's eye cane on the faces of each bead slice, front and back. Insert a hole through the bead from top to bottom with the needle tool. Make two beads for each shape, or as many beads as you wish to place in the design.

7. Bake all of the pieces.

8. Insert an eye pin into each bead. Turn the extruding pin into a loop (Fig. 6).

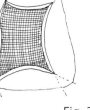

Fig. 6

9. Use a bail as a "hanger" and clamp onto the mobile shapes where desired. Use jump rings to attach the bails to the beads and to the hanging mobiles.

10. Attach the pieces one at a time as you balance the mobile. You can hang the mobile from the ceiling with fishing line or a chain.

Shapes in Space

This vessel is decorated with lines and shapes. The background is the space the shapes are in (the negative space). Depending upon where you place your shapes, the vessel can have a completely different appearance; for example, the lips and spirals could be alternating and placed to create a border. This vessel was designed to hold lipstick, but you can alter the height and width to create any size form you wish.

Materials

2 bricks black Fimo soft glitter*
2 bricks red clay
1/4 brick gold clay
9" x 4-1/2" WireForm mesh sparkle aluminum
Jeweler's buffing wheel or soft polishing cloth
400, 600, and 800 grit wet sandpaper
Blade, roller, pasta machine, card stock, paper, scissors, "lips template," varnish (optional)

*This is the only clay with glitter in the formulation
Note: Vessel can be gloss varnished instead of polished

1. Condition (setting 3) and prepare one sheet glitter clay and one sheet red clay, each approximately 10" long by 5" high.

2. Place the red sheet of clay on a piece of card stock.

3. Place the mesh on the clay and embed it into the surface with the roller. The mesh should fit just inside the edge of the clay.

4. Now place the glitter sheet of clay on top of the red, and try not to create air bubbles as the mesh gets buried between the two sheets (Fig. 1).

5. Draw and cut out a paper "lips" pattern—it can even be your own lips! (Fig. 2)

6. Flatten a thin sheet of red clay and place the lips pattern on the clay. Cut several patterns of lips and place on the sparkle clay. Next, make a very thin snake of gold clay and spiral the clay on the surface of the sparkle clay in several places (Fig. 3)

7. Roll the entire surface flush, embedding the shapes and spirals into the sparkle clay.

8. On the right side edge of the work, remove the top clay 1/2" off of the mesh. On the left side edge, remove the bottom clay 1/2" off of the mesh (Fig. 4).

9. On the top edge, trim and straighten the edge evenly but not down to where the mesh will show through. You will trim the bottom in Step 11.

10. Pick up the slab and, with the red side of the work on the inside, join the edges, overlapping where you have removed the clay in Step 8. Adjust as needed and press the edges together. Stand the work on end and bend the ends (seam at midpoint) so that it is an elongated oval. Creating a bend in the oval will help to keep the form from springing apart and have less pressure on the seams. You can always widen it if needed. With your fingers, gently press the overlapped edges to secure the seams. Reinforce the seam inside of the cylinder with another thin strip of red clay. Smooth the seams (Fig. 5).

11. When the desired form is straight and even, trim the clay at the bottom, flush with the mesh; this will help reinforce the vessel as it is attached to the bottom.

12. Prepare a sheet of thick red clay (two stacked sheets of thickness from Step 1) to serve as the base of the vessel. Place the work on the base and press the vessel into it firmly to secure. Trim the base to the shape of the vessel. You can also "bevel" the bottom by trimming it while holding the blade at a slight angle.

13. Bake and cool the vessel. Polish or gloss the vessel with varnish if desired.

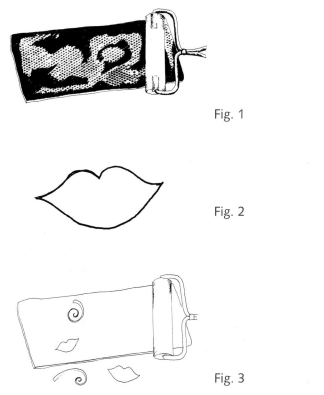

Fig. 1

Fig. 2

Fig. 3

Fig. 4

Fig. 5

Chapter 8
Line and Space

A line is one of the most common forms of visual communication. For instance, attention to lines keeps us from crashing into each other on the road. The elements and principles of art are important not only in our designs but in our lives as well. We form a human line at the grocery checkout to wait our turn, and the image of a cigarette, inside of a red circle with a diagonal line, is a universal sign for "no smoking." Line also has to do with space. Space—with a line around it—becomes a shape. Stripes have a certain amount of space between the lines. The amount of space, the color of space, and the placement of shapes within space are important considerations in design. The following information presents line and space as elements that have purpose in a design.

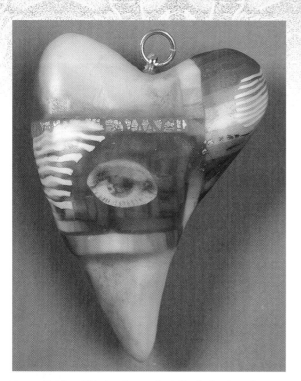

Linnea Tobias. This lovely pendant illustrates how line helps organize the design.

Lion and Zebra. Line drawings by Robby McGuire carved in polymer clay by Barbara A. McGuire.

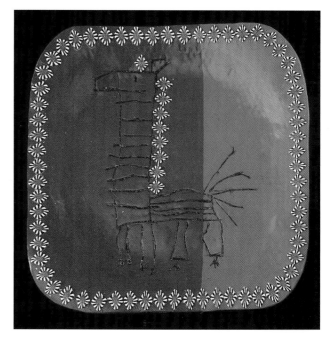

$\mathcal{L}$*ine*

Tory Hughes

George Post

Above: "Japanese Shrimp" by Tory Hughes. Hughes uses line to create dynamic movement in her composition.

Right: Susan Hyde. This dynamic work of art incorporates many applications of color and borders as lines.

Line is one of the most obvious elements of design, but the complete family of what can be described as line may not be so obvious. In polymer clay, lines gain another dimension; physical edges become lines. A line is not always made of ink; it can be embossing powder or a groove of carved clay.

A line is actually a point, dot, or succession of dots. It has a thickness and length and moves in a direction. The continuation from point A to point B is infinitely variable—it does not have to be straight to be a line. Nor does it have to be black to be a line. A line can be an object or a division. It can be texture and it can describe a shape or form. Contour lines describe a shape in simple

form. Disconnected lines or overlapping lines may describe varying planes.

Lines are very important because they are leaders. They lead our eyes and evoke stimulation. Lines indicate movement. Horizontal lines, those lying flat and going from side to side, evoke calmness and stability. This is understandable when we consider the earth's gravity and our balance when we are lying down. Invisible horizontal lines help organize letters into words. Vertical lines go up and down and imply height or organization. They lead our eye up and down on a page. There are invisible vertical lines that organize text into columns.

Diagonal lines slant and usually evoke a feeling of movement or tension. Zigzags are diagonal lines that change direction and may indicate agitated or irregular movement. Straight lines can be hard, sharp, rigid, and grounding. Curved lines are bent and can be rhythmic, flowing, organic, and soft. When short gaps are placed between lines in a directional pattern, our eye will fill in the blanks; this is referred to as closure. Lines are the basic tools of organization in a work of art. Each line is an essential element, yet an extra line is inefficient and overbearing.

Is a spiral a line? Yes—and a powerful line at that! A spiral is perhaps one of the most pleasing and identifiable lines in nature because of its rhythmic proportion. It also can convey expression in the direction of its opening and the tightness of its winding.

Right: Mike Buesseler. This beautiful locket uses line to lead the eye through the composition.

Below: Hearts by Evelyn Gibson. The varying thickness of the lines in Gibson's translucent and white hearts gives the pattern a romantic, as opposed to rigid, decorative style.

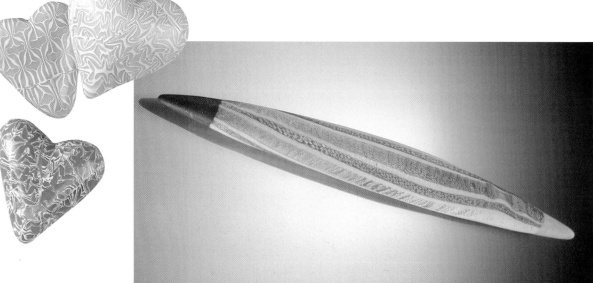

Ralph Gabriner

"Chrysalis Brooche Sherbert Frost Series" by Elise Winters. Elegant flowing lines give movement to this sleek form.

"Heart Spiral" by Celie Fago. Fago has incredible talent for utilizing the simplicity of an elegant line.

 Heartfelt Lines

There are many options in discovering lines. These simple pins or magnets explore applied lines, edges, borders, and form representing line.

Materials

Small amounts of three colors of clay (see Step 1)
Small shape cookie cutter, texture, cornstarch, blade, special edge scissors (optional), magnet or pin back, super glue, thin line permanent marker, pasta machine

1. Choose three colors of clay, one for the background, one for the cut-out, and one for the applied line. There should be contrast in the colors for definition

2. Condition a sheet (about 1/8" thick) of background clay and a sheet of the cut-out clay, each 3" x 3" square.

3. Create a textured background. Choose a simple texture, like a screen or woven cloth. Brush a very small amount of cornstarch on the sheet's flat surface to prepare the clay for texture. Press the texture material gently into the clay and release, leaving a slight impression in the clay (Fig. 1). Set aside.

Fig. 1

4. Using the cookie cutter, cut a shape (like the heart or house shown in the photo) out of the contrast color (Fig. 2).

Fig. 2

5. Roll a thin snake out of the "line" clay (it doesn't have to be an even thickness if you wish!). Secure one end of the snake to the shape made in Step 4 and "draw" on the surface (a spiral is shown). Press gently to secure the position of the clay line (uncured clay will stick to itself) (Fig. 3). You can also

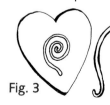
Fig. 3

create textured "line" by impressing tools into the clay.

6. Place the cut shape on the background.

Fig. 4

7. Trim the entire piece; the edges will frame the work. (The example at top was cut with a cookie cutter and then trimmed with a pinking shears. A zigzag strip was placed next to the shape (Fig. 4).

8. You can use another "snake" to border the piece. To make a striped border, twist three strands of clay together and roll smooth. Continue twisting to tighten the stripe (Fig. 5).

Fig. 5

9. Bake the piece. A magnet or pin back can be glued on with super glue after baking.

10. Sign your work on the back with a thin line permanent marker.

*B*lended Bead Shells

In this exercise, you will create a line without actually drawing one! The edge where the spiral rolls onto itself creates a line, and the applied canes also create a line. The cord on which the pendant is hung is a line that intersects the form. It is also interesting to note that although we have used two colors in the samples shown, there is no distinct "line" between them.

Materials

1/2 block clay any color (Fimo transparent 01 shown)
1/2 block clay any color (Fimo green-gold shown)
1/2 block clay white (scrap clay can also be used)
Cane slices (for ideas, see pages 67, 100, and 108)
30" leather cord
Blade, roller, large-diameter needle tool, pasta machine

1. Make two tall right triangles, the same size, of each color that will cover the surface of the finished bead. Flip and invert one of the triangles vertically. Place the triangle's base to point, flush to each other, with the diagonal adjacent (as in the Skinner Blend described on page 53).

2. Fold the rectangle in half vertically. Note: Never turn the fold the opposite way. You will get a mix of the two colors, not a graduation.

3. Run it through the pasta machine. Note: If you don't have a pasta machine you can do this technique by rolling and stretching the slab out with your hands. Hold one end and tug as you roll smooth (it may take a little practice).

4. Keep folding the rectangle in half vertically and running it through the pasta machine until the color is blended. It may take ten to fifteen times through the press to get it even.

5. Cover an oval form of white (or scrap) clay, about 2" long by 3/4" in diameter, with the shaded clay (one color at each end) (Fig. 1).

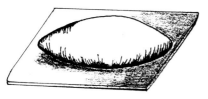

Fig. 1

6. Roll the clay into a point at each end (Fig.2). Starting at the point, wind the cone into a spiral. Wind the opposite point into a spiral going in the opposite direction (or you can flatten it after you have sealed the end).

Fig. 2

7. Condition and reduce the decorative cane as directed on the package (if purchased). Slice the cane into thin disks and apply by pressing to the surface of the bead in rings as shown or as desired (Fig.3).

Fig. 3

8. Accounting for the balance of the weight in the bead, suspend the bead between two fingers as if it where being "held" by the cord. Mark the place where the cord should be inserted. Pierce the bead horizontally through the width of the form with a large-diameter needle tool.

9. Bake bead and string on the leather cord.

Space

George Post

Above: "Raven Necklace" by Margaret Regan. Attention is drawn to the shapes in this design by Regan's dynamic use of contrast and positive and negative space.

Right: Susan Kraus. The use of negative space in this design adds beautiful, refined definition to the shape of the elk.

Space is an element that relates to focus and how objects are perceived in depth. We refer to positive space as the object and negative space to the area that surrounds it. This can change depending upon the context of the focal point, as in a ring of concentric circles. Space is also two- or three-dimensional. Actual space is three-dimensional; it is volume that is empty or filled. Space in a picture is perceived, an illusion and only suggested by the placement and relationship of objects. But, these suggestions are very real because our mind is willing to accept the implied communication.

When a shape is placed in front of or on top of another shape, we get a feeling of depth. When an element is placed higher on a page, it seems to be farther back in the perspective of the picture. This also happens when things are diminishing in size. Perspective describes the spatial depth of an image. Perspective emphasizes what is closest to the viewer, although this is an illusion in a two-dimensional piece. One-point perspective is when you are viewing something straight on, where the

Above: "Topiary Garden" by Tory Hughes. The smaller tree shapes placed higher in the composition help give the illusion of depth. The images on the postage stamp also reflect a classic two-point perspective.

Left: Varda Levram-Ellisman. This translucent cane design has effectively utilized a relationship in size, bringing the largest flower forward.

entire plane of an object is directly in view. Two-point perspective is when you are viewing something on an angle or corner so the form recedes into space, creating volume and depth. Color and value give large contributions to depth (think of shadows). When a painter highlights an image, it usually brings that plane or form to the front. But on the same note, objects placed in the distance may be lighter in value and less intense and detailed, because they seem to diminish.

"Landscapes" by Mike Buesseler.
Buesseler is a master of spatial
relation as shown in his incredible
landscape designs.

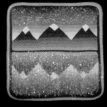

Space also communicates time and movement. If you have a figure leaping off the edge of a building, the bottom of the landing and the time it takes to reach it are in relationship to the amount of space between the jumper and the ground. The movement of a bouncing ball can be communicated by the amount of space between bounces. Indeed, if you place a ball at the edge of a page, it looks like it is bouncing off into space.

Space is also a resting point for the eye; elements in a design need some space to communicate. Just as we need space to move physically, pictures on a wall need some space between them to be appreciated individually. If there is a lot of space around an object, attention is drawn to it. When you have too many images or elements in a design, you don't have enough space.

Right: "Mermaid & Angel" by Svetlana Vovina. These delightful figures seem to float due to the space that surrounds them.

Below: "Geoclock" by Cassie Doyon. Large amounts of space in this design allow the simplicity of a few geometric shapes to communicate clearly.

"Iowa Autumn" by Patricia Kimle. The space in the village scene gives a feeling of a small farm nestled in a large open area. This egg was displayed at the White House Easter festivities in 1998.

Patricia Kimle

Space Puzzle

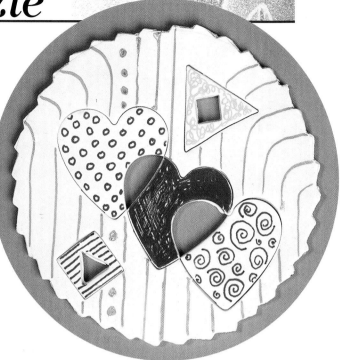

This simple and fun-to-make puzzle illustrates positive and negative space. It is also a good chance to experiment with surface treatments, such as pencils, powders, glitters, and markers.

Materials

1 block white clay*
Small shape cutters or Kemper tool cutters
Card stock, special edge scissors (optional)
Identi-pens, Prisma colored pencils, Sakura Pen-Touch Gold, pasta machine
*The clay used in this project was Fimo soft, primarily because of its compatibility for use with colored markers.

1. Condition and flatten a sheet of white clay about 5" x 5" square. It is helpful to work directly on a card stock work surface that can be placed in the oven.

2. Using a few small cookie cutters or Kemper tool cutters, press and cut a design into the clay. Widen the design slightly by shimmying the cutters. This will make it easier to separate. Cross the cutters, or make cut-outs inside of cut-outs (Fig. 1 and 2).

Fig. 1

Fig. 2

3. Pull a few of the smaller cut pieces completely out of the art, creating blank space. This will help you to be able to pick up the pieces when the puzzle is completely done (Fig. 3).

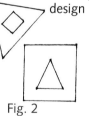

Fig. 3

4. Bake the pieces.

5. When the pieces are cool, decide on the edge and shape of the puzzle. In the example shown, a circle was cut out with special edge scissors (Fig. 4). (You can also cut the puzzle before it is baked, but cutting after baking gives you a little more control and less distortion of the puzzle pieces and how they fit.)

Fig. 4

6. Using Prisma colored pencils or a Sakura pen, draw designs on the puzzle pieces and the background (Fig.5). The gold background shown was done with a Sakura Pen-Touch Gold.

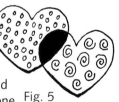

Fig. 5

*F*rame Within a Frame

The object of this exercise is to draw attention to the focal point by manipulating the space around it. As each layer is added, it brings that layer to the front and suggests that the original layer recedes. Also, the amount of surface area in the layers gives enough space for that layer to be effective in balancing the piece.

Materials

5" x 5" piece of solid, neutral-colored base clay
Several sheets of colored clay
Magic Leaf (Burnished leaf)
Fimo Varnish (for leaf)
Letter stamps (spells TIME in photo)
Watch face
Pearl
Texture, cornstarch
Roller, blade, acrylic paint (optional), pasta machine

1. Choose a tiny focal element. It can be an image, sculpture, word, button, or jewel. In the example shown, the focal point is the word "TIME."

2. Condition a flat sheet of solid neutral-colored clay, something that contrasts, but does not compete, with the image.

3. Place the object (or image) somewhere on the sheet of clay other than the center. In this example, the word "TIME" was pressed into the clay.

4. Begin to build a frame around the focal point by layering different colors of conditioned, torn (or straight) sheets, overlapping and withdrawing from the focal point toward the edge of the piece. These sheets can be textured (see Chapter 2) or have a surface treatment like the gold leaf shown in the example. (To apply gold leaf to the clay, simply lay the leaf across the clay and roll smooth. There is a natural adhesion to the clay. If the clay separates during rolling, a crackle design will appear in the surface.)

5. Add smaller bits or objects, such as the watch face and the pearl shown, to create interest and balance the composition (Fig. 1).

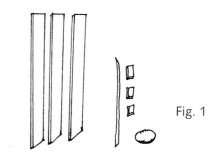

Fig. 1

6. By the time you are finished you will have several layers of clay stacked on top of each other, especially at the outer edges. Trim the outer edges with the blade to create an interesting shape. Finish the piece by beveling the stack as shown (Fig. 2). This is done by slanting the blade at an angle as you trim the clay.

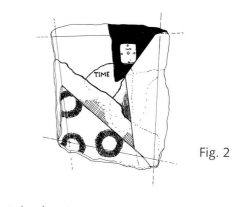

Fig. 2

7. Bake the piece.

8. If desired, after the piece has cooled, you can color the textured areas with acrylic paint, filling the indentations and wiping off the excess. This is how the word "TIME" was defined in the example.

9. To finish, you may wish to frame this collage or use it as a cover for a book.

Chapter 9

texture

Texture refers to the dimension or tactile character of a surface, both simulated and actual. Simulated texture is surface design, like a drawing, that gives the illusion of texture, whereas actual texture is three-dimensional, because it is a physical variation of the surface. Texture carries a unique impact because it can be felt as well as seen. This adds a sensual quality to the communication in the design. Texture suggests the characteristics of materials such as cloth, wood, glass, or bone. It can be the interrelated network of individual components to create a whole, such as brick creating the texture of a chimney or reeds creating the texture of a basket. In this chapter, we will look at the different kinds of texture available to a polymer clay artist and how to use texture as an element of design to give the work personality.

Toni Belonogoff. Simulated texture unifies the composition presented in this silk-screened and metallic leaf pin.

Wireart by Chris Gluck. The creative use of wire gives lively texture to this colorful necklace

"Japan Dolls" by Emi Fukushima. Texture is applied to simulate hair and cloth in these charming Japanese doll pendants.

George Post

"Drum Beads" by Karen Lewis of Klew Expressions. Lewis applies detailed cane slices to the surface of her beads to create interesting texture and rhythm in her design.

Lines can also be texture. Carved lines are an obvious example of this. Edges can also become texture, and stacked texture can create depth. Applied dots can create texture and pattern at the same time. Rough texture can appear harsh, coarse, or scratchy. A finely-sanded texture is velvety and soft. When the texture is buffed or varnished, it appears glossy and smooth.

Even a small bit of texture or simulated texture can add interest and dimension to a composition. Texture breaks the "flatness" of shape and monotony of large surface areas. Too much texture gets confusing or boring, and the eye searches for relief. Therefore, texture, as with all elements, is a planned enhancement and serves an exact purpose.

"Ginko Leaf" by Nan Roche. Texture was imprinted onto the surface of these designs. Roche developed this mokume gane technique using the matrix of rubber stamps.

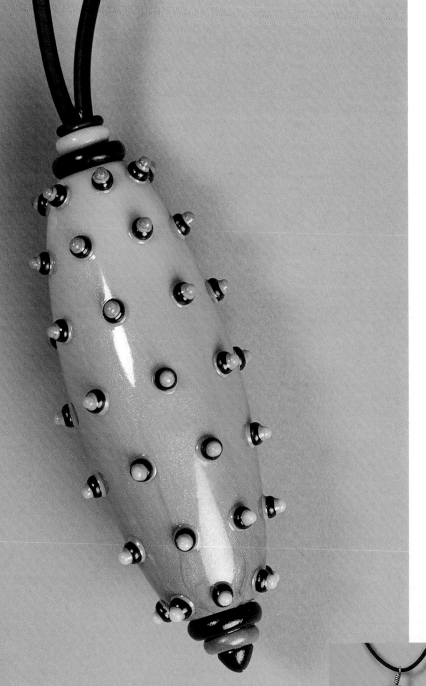

Above: Susan Kraus. This beautiful pendant bead utilizes the dynamic texture of the applied forms as emphasis to the design.

Right: Jeni Fiske. This sculpted bead has subtle texture that places emphasis on the form.

Texture reflects light; hence, texture creates value contrast in the surface of the form. This is why texture is so visually impacting.

Because polymer clay is an exceptional molding material, it duplicates the surface of nearly any texture. Your home may be a treasure trove of texture, such as cloth, baskets, plastics, and rubber stamps. Create your own texture by carving or imprinting shapes, patterns, lines—anything imaginable. You can even create texture with natural objects like a real leaf! Luckily, Mother Nature is copyright-free!

"Evening Star" by Violette Laporte. This quilt composition offers a pleasing and interesting use of texture, both actual and implied.

Violette Laporte

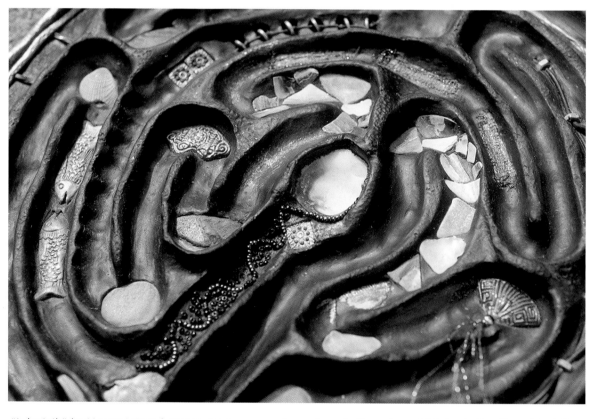

"Labyrinth" by Margaret Kristof. Texture creates a sensual experience in the surface of this fascinating finger labyrinth.

Buttons by Marie Johannes. The texture in these vintage replica buttons creates changes in value, enabling the eye to see details.

The House that Margaret Built

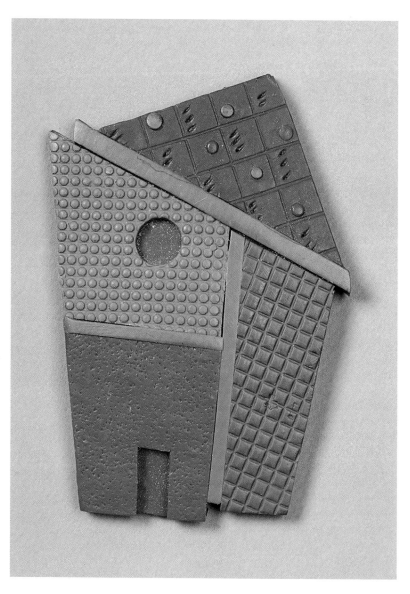

The sample shown here and project idea are presented through the generosity of Margaret Maggio. This delightful little house is a great way to experiment with texture. Notice which textures seem to complement each other and the movement created by the line direction in the textures.

Materials

Five polymer clay colors*
1/4 block black clay
Textures (see Step 2 for ideas)
Pin back
Cornstarch, tracing paper, pencil, scissors, soft paint brush, blade, roller, pasta machine
*Three options (Fig. 1-3) are shown below; choose one for the project. Use the five colors in any arrangement you find pleasing.

1. Condition very small amounts of each of the five colors. Condition the black clay to serve as the base. Roll this into a flat sheet, approximately the size of the finished "house."

2. Roll the colored clay into small flat sheets. Brush the clay very lightly with cornstarch or an alternative powder to act as a release. Imprint with texture (Fig. 4), such as:
• button imprints in a grid pattern
• carved ring rolled across clay
• Lego toy building blocks
• plastic needlework canvas
• plastic reflector imprint
• rubber stamp impression
• screen
• straight lines imprinted with a knitting needle
• woven cloth
• WireForm mesh
• wood grain

3. Trace a "house" from one of the illustrations. Cut out the individual pieces to use as patterns.

4. Arrange the patterns on the textured sheets as desired (Fig. 5). Make your own decision as to which patterns go on which colors and/or textures of clay. Trim the clay according to the patterns with a sharp knife.

5. Arrange the cut shapes according to the original pattern on the black base sheet of clay to build the house (Fig. 6).

6. Bake the house face down. Attach the pin back using a small rectangle of textured clay to hold it in place.

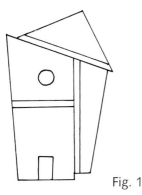

Fig. 1

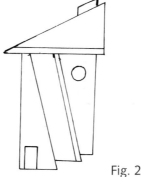

Fig. 2

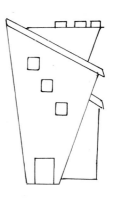

Fig. 3

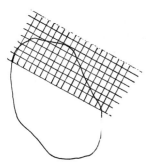

Fig. 4

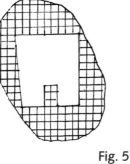

Fig. 5

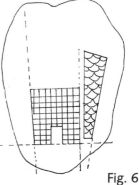

Fig. 6

Texture City

This town is made of simulated drawn texture. The accuracy of the texture drawings is not important; it is a good exercise to play with scribbles, lines, and pattern. The implied texture will add character to the buildings. Notice the placement of solid pieces to balance the design and rest the eye from the active movement of the line in the texture.

Materials

*Five polymer clay colors, pastel or bright colors of light value, enough to create the buildings (see Step 1)
1/4 block light, neutral gray clay
Tracing paper, white paper, pencil, pen, roller, blade, rubbing alcohol, Q-tip, pin back, super glue, photocopier, magnet (optional), pasta machine*

1. Condition the colored clay. Condition the gray clay to serve as the background and roll it into a 4" square flat sheet, approximately the size of the finished "city" (use Fig. 1 as a guide to draw your city).

Fig. 1

2. Roll the colored clay into flat sheets. Set aside.

3. Trace the city outline patterns given or invent your own outline patterns on a piece of white paper (Fig. 2).

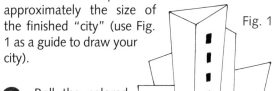

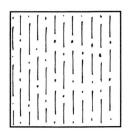

Fig. 2

4. Draw the texture onto the buildings (directly on the tracing paper or white paper). The windows are penciled in. Ideas for drawing simulated textures are:
• drawn stripes in different values
• feathers
• rubber stamp impressions
• sand
• scales
• scribbling
• spirals and helixes
• waves
• wood grain
• woven cloth

5. Photocopy the "city" with the texture you have just drawn. The copier you choose should be of good quality and produce a clear image (Fig. 3). (Note: Your photocopy will be a reverse image.)

Fig. 3

6. Cut the city buildings apart. Place them ink side down on the clay sheets, deciding which buildings will go on which colors. Cut out the pieces with a blade (Fig. 4).

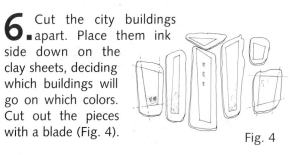

Fig. 4

7. Apply rubbing alcohol with a Q-tip to the back side of the paper (this helps release the ink). Bake.

8. Peel the images off the buildings.

9. Arrange the buildings according to the design of your original outline pattern on the flat sheet of gray clay.

10. Bake again.

11. Glue a pin back (or magnet if desired) on with super glue .

Chapter 10
Balance, Pattern, and Rhythm

The following three concepts—balance, pattern and rhythm—are grouped together because most repetitions employ the logic of balance and create a sequential "flow" or rhythm. There are obvious applications of each of the these principles. Two objects that are the same, evenly spaced, are balanced. When something is duplicated, in an adjacent sequence, a pattern results. A series of shapes, just like musical notes, has a beat or rhythm. This chapter discusses what is not obvious, such as unlike objects being balanced, or how an altered sequence can create an invented series of shapes, or how rhythm can be reflected in a subtle surface texture. A design need not be complicated or decorated to employ these principles. An artist who incorporates these principles (consciously or subconsciously) into his or her work will achieve quality and depth in the design.

Above: "Jester" by Margi Laurin. This charming character's arms and legs are just the right proportion and placement to balance the form.

Right: Karen and Ann Mitchell. The sisters of AnKara Designs have incredible balance in their sensational filigree jewelry. Their skillful choice of color and accentuating use of clay enhance their unique designs.

Balance

Ted Brobst

Above: "Star Beads" by Jane Brobst. Brobst was awarded the 1997 Embellishments Award for these original designs which explore the use of radial symmetry.

Balance is perhaps one of the most crucial principles of design, because it refers to the visual weight of the elements and their distribution in a composition. When we are out of balance, we fall. When a design is out of balance, something is unsettling. In jewelry design, for example, a pendant that is too big or heavy for the cord does not look right. If a strand of beads overbears the centerpiece, its impact or attention is diminished—the design goal has not been accomplished and it loses potential appeal.

There are many types of balance, all of which enable endless variety and interest. The most obvious is symmetry, in which objects appearing to be of equal weight are on either side of a central axis. A mirror image is absolute symmetry. If the elements radiate out from a central point, it is called radial symmetry. Many flowers are examples of radial symmetry, as are the wedges of an orange. Symmetrical balance communicates stability and order, both in nature and design.

Above: Marie Segal. The variation in texture adds interest to the symmetrical design in this bug pendant.

Left: Nuchi Draimen. This pin displays a floral motif based on radial symmetry.

"Dragonfly" by Margaret Regan. The focal point (the dragonflies) on this pin appears to be slightly off-balance. This, however, may have been intentional placement by the artist to create movement in the piece.

Asymmetry is when different elements balance each other visually. If a person were to extend a right arm and a left leg, depending on the angle, visual, and, in this example, physical weight, balance could be achieved. The same applies to design. Different elements carry different visual weight. Blank space has visual weight and texture has visual weight. A group of small shapes can visually balance a large shape. A trained eye will also asses weight in color and value. A rather intense color, or contrasting color, carries a visual weight depending upon its context. A shape with dark value generally carries more weight given it is on a light background. If the same shape is on a similar value background, it will lose its visual weight. In this respect, contrast carries visual weight. A small irregular shape can balance a large smooth one. The size of an object also reflects visual weight.

Sometimes it is intentional that a piece be out of balance to create tension. But, whatever the goal, the quality of the design should lie in the strength of the composition and the character of the elements, as opposed to intentional balance.

Right: Vessel by Dan Cormier. Cormier utilizes symmetry of form in his perfectly balanced work.

Right: "Mezzuah Swap" by Barbara A. McGuire, Varda Levram-Ellison, and Lisa Pavelka. Each work employs a different application of balance.

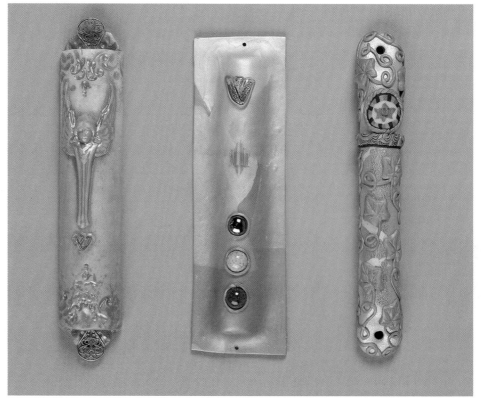

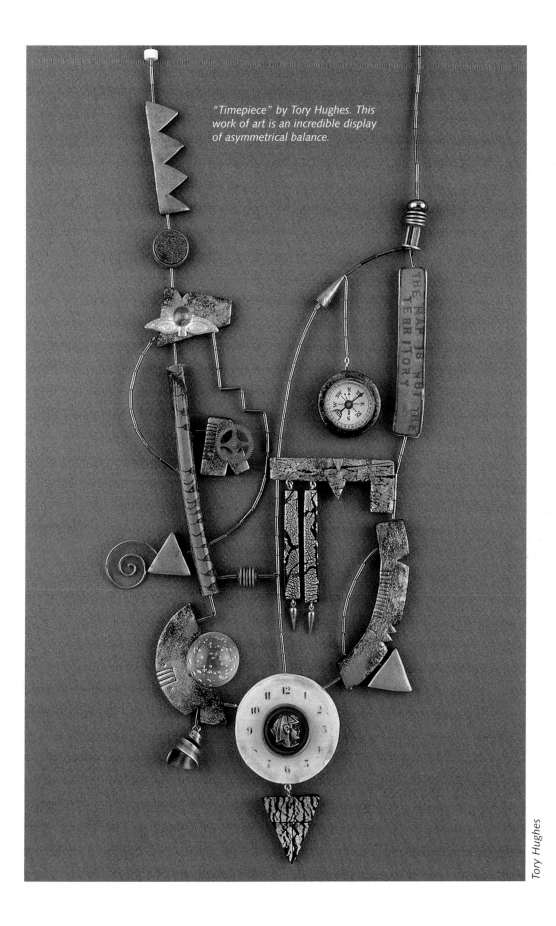

"Timepiece" by Tory Hughes. This work of art is an incredible display of asymmetrical balance.

Tory Hughes

Balanced Barrettes

These barrettes may be more challenging than they appear. The size and shape of the canes can be arranged in an infinite variety of sequences. When you arrange the canes, notice how some sequences just do or don't look "right." That is because the visual weight of an element also refers to its context. Each barrette is built on an additional layer of clay. This serves to balance the activity on the top as well as finish the edge, adding another "frame" to the composition.

Materials

1/4 block of two colors of clay (similar or neutral, top photo; contrasting, bottom photo)
Assorted canes*
Barrette back
Roller, blade, super glue, pasta machine

*You may either use canes from other projects in this book, including the Radial Cane and Patterned Egg projects (see pages 100 and 106, respectively), or for simplicity you can use pre-made canes such as KaliedoKane designer canes (shown in bottom photo).

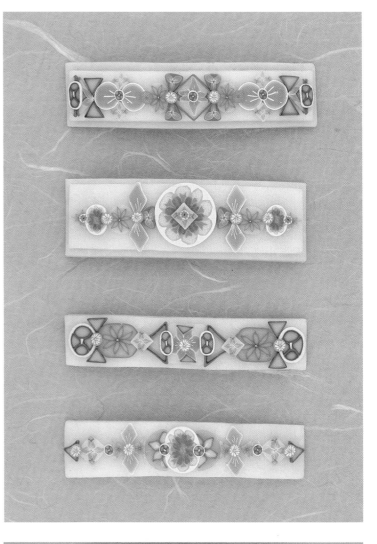

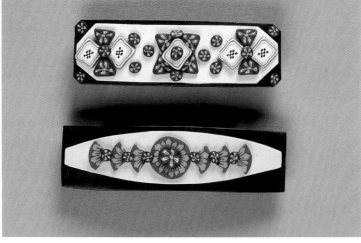

1. Make or choose two or three simple canes to decorate your barrette.

2. Condition the canes by "massaging" until flexible; that is, roll back and forth in your palms and squeeze, pushing end to end. This softens the cane for further use.

3. Reduce the canes, as desired, by rolling or pinching. Work slowly so you do not crack the cane (Fig. 1).

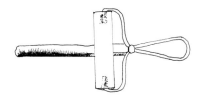

Fig. 1

4. Pinch the cane into different shapes such as a triangle, square, or diamond. You can also cut the slices into half circles, quarters, or strips.

5. Slice the cane with a sharp blade into thin, even slices that will decorate the barrette (Fig. 2).

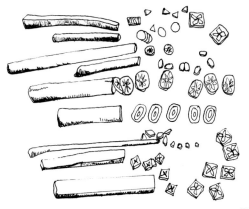

Fig. 2

6. Pick a neutral color and roll a thin sheet (setting 4). Cut a rectangle, approximately 3" by 5" long, that will serve as a preliminary base. You will trim it after the design is completely finished.

7. Arrange the cane slices, starting with a midpoint and extending them out toward the edges. You can stack the canes if desired. Don't press them in too hard so you can still move

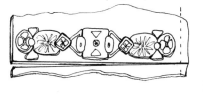

Fig. 3

them around. When you have your final arrangement, press evenly to secure the slices.

8. Trim the base in the shape you desire (Fig. 3).

9. Make another base of a contrasting or similar color and place the designed piece on top. Trim this base.

10. Bake the barrette directly on top of the barrette back. This will allow for the barrette's curve.

11. When cool, pop off the barrette back. Apply super glue and re-place on barrette.

Radial Flower Cane

This is an exercise in radial symmetry and is also a popular way to build canes. This flower is symmetrical because the number of petals is even. You can use the cane to make beads as shown, but slices of the cane can be used to decorate any polymer clay surface area (see Balanced Barrette project, page 98 as an example).

Materials

1 block pastel color clay
1/2 block clay similar color (to the pastel color)
1/2 block clay outline color (with contrast)*
1 block neutral color clay
Small snake of dark color
Roller, blade, needle tool, pasta machine
* White outlines will really pop the design out.
Note: The clay should be a firm clay suitable for caning, such as Fimo.

1. Choose your color theme and condition the clay. The whole effect of the cane depends upon the contrast or subtle blending of the colors.

You will need two similar flower petal colors, an outline color (contrasting), and a background color (neutral).

2. Start with a large tube of pastel colored clay, approximately 4" long by 1/2" in diameter.

3. Wrap with an additional (similar) color of clay (Fig. 1). Make sure the edges meet exactly to create a smooth, even layer around the core (Fig. 2).

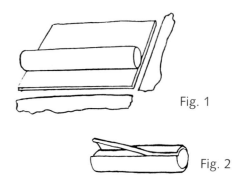

Fig. 1

Fig. 2

4. Wrap a third, ultra-thin layer (the outline color); this will outline the flower.

5. Reduce the cane by rolling it with even pressure. It will increase in length as it decreases in diameter. When it is a length of 12", roll it flat with the roller, or pinch it into a flat cylinder with pointed edges (Fig. 3, 4,5).

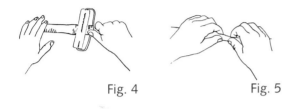

Fig. 3

Fig. 4   Fig. 5

6. Cut the cylinder into eight or more pieces, about 1-1/2" long.

7. Place these pieces, standing upright on end, around a tiny snake of contrasting colored clay (Fig. 6).

Fig. 6

8. You will now fill in the gaps between the petals (this is considered the negative space). Roll another cylinder (the background color) about 1-1/2" long, with the width about the same size as the upright petals. This color is the flower's background.

9. Cut this cylinder from top to bottom into a pie (you will need the same number of pieces as there are petals) (Fig. 7).

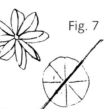

Fig. 7

10. Pinch the pie sections to fit into the gaps

between the petals. Trim the excess with a blade if it extends past the border (Fig. 8).

Fig. 8

11. Wrap the new cane with an additional layer the same color as the negative space, or background (Fig. 9).

Fig. 9

12. Gently pack the cane and reduce it to the desired diameter. You may wish to cut the cane into different lengths and reduce (as described above) each length to a different diameter to increase design options.

13. Store the cane by wrapping it with a sheet of heavy plastic (freezer bag-type) or wax paper. Use an airtight container to hold all of your uncured canes and clay. When you are ready to use the cane again, simply roll it gently in your palms to take the stiffness out of it. Reduce further if desired, slice, and apply to your particular project.

14. Making a bead: Roll a ball of solid color clay slightly smaller than the size you desire the bead to be. Place thin slices of the cane on top of the bead in random or planned patterns. Once the designs are placed, roll the bead back and forth in the palms of your hands to embed the cane slices into the surface. Using a needle tool, poke a hole through the bead. When the tool starts to emerge from the opposite side, reverse and poke through again. This prevents a protrusion at the hole. Bake with one of the holes down on the baking surface to help eliminate a flat spot (Fig. 10).

Fig. 10

Pattern

George Post

Patricia Kimle

Top: Sarah Shriver. Shriver excels in connecting shape and line to create interlocking patterns.

Above: "Starbust" by Patricia Kimle. Kimle balances the weight of this beautiful, precise pattern with a random pattern of gold leaf mokume gane.

Right: "Laugh and the World Laughs with You" card by Audrey Forcier. Invisible underlying grids establish the placement of images and shapes that create the pattern in this design. Forcier's work is part of Polymer Clay Art Cards by Colorado Card and Curiosity.

Pattern is the repetition of lines, shapes, or textures that organizes to form an overall design. Repetitions can be found in sequences or alternates. Patterns can be planned or random and are easily found in nature; for example, a honeycomb has a hexagon pattern, a dahlia a radial pattern, zebras have an irregular striped pattern, and certain snakes are cloaked in a beautiful diamond pattern.

The basic understructure or grid of patterns is called the network. In *The Principles of Pattern Design*, Richard M. Proctor classifies pattern structure and organization into square, brick, half drop, diamond, triangle, ogee, hexagon, and scale. When shapes, lines, and images are contained within a certain unit and that unit is repeated, patterns evolve (these are the details inside). As the individual units are flipped, rotated, turned, or connected, a variation or more complex pattern may emerge.

Kenji Kerins

Not all patterns repeat the same motif. Variety adds interest to the theme or design in the pattern. Patterns can alternate images or the size of images. Value adds depth and variety to patterns.

Texture is commonly used in pattern. The shadows of a textured surface pattern add another dimension to visual stimulation. Because polymer clay is so adaptable to molding and imprinting, it is easy to employ a common texture such as a button or rubber stamp and imprint a pattern in the clay.

Sharon Ohlhorst. Ohlhorst experimented with pattern after reading instructions from Sandra McCaw that were printed in the polymer clay newsletter PolyInformer.

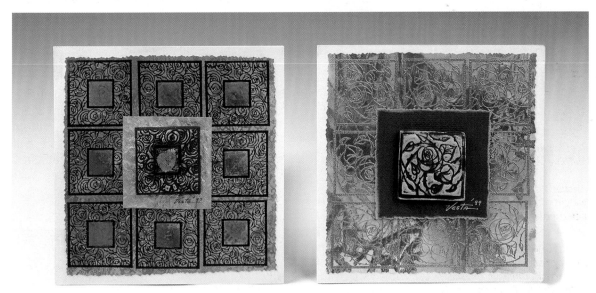

Cards by Debra Donovan of Commotion—The Art of Rubber Stamping. Donovan imprints a pattern on paper as a border and creates unity by repeating the pattern in the polymer clay at the center of the design.

Jeff Baird

Sandra McCaw. These patterns connect to create depth and optical illusions because of their change in value.

Eggs by Carol L. Simmons. These beautiful eggs were created by interlocking the cane patterns.

One of the most popular and intriguing techniques in working with polymer clay is creating a cane. Canes are long cylinders of clay that have a design built into them that continues the entire length of the cylinder. Repeated forms are usually employed in the actual building of a cane although it need not be the only basis for design. Once a cane is built, it can be cut into many equal lengths and then reassembled to create more complex designs or patterns in the new cane. Also, canes need not be constantly reassembled as new canes; single slices from one cane can be arranged on a surface, interconnecting or in a sequence. This is of huge advantage in decoration, for pattern not only decorates the surface but also adds rhythm and movement to the art.

Intricate Patterned Eggs

Eggs are a fun way to experiment with pattern. This exercise uses applied canes to create complex patterns. Open areas of the egg, not covered with canes, can also be incorporated into the design. You may either use canes from other projects in the book, including the Radial Flower Cane, Bull's Eye Cane, or Spiked Center Cane (see pages 100, 108, and 67 respectively), or for simplicity, you can use pre-made canes such as KaliedoKane designer canes.

Materials

1/2 block pastel color clay*
1/4 block similar color clay (to the pastel)
1/4 block white clay
Blown-out egg or papier mâché egg
Sobo Glue, needle tool
*Fimo clay is used here because the thin slices must retain their shape to keep the pattern neat and even.

1. Start with either a blown-out or papier mâché egg. If using a blown-out one, wash and let dry. Coat the entire egg with Sobo Glue and let dry.

Fig. 1

2. Choose several canes that have compatible colors or themes. Pinch, press, or roll these canes into various diameters and interesting shapes such as triangles, wedges, or diamonds.

3. Slice several canes into small pieces.

4. Arrange the slices, building from the north, south, east, and west around the egg. Once these initial points are centered you can build a pattern and rings of pattern (Fig. 1).

5. When you place a cane over the "blown-out" hole of a real egg, lift it slightly to allow air to release while baking.

6. Bake the egg.

Spiked Center Cane

Note: The beginning of these instructions is the same as Radial Flower Cane (see page 100). It is typical for canes to be built in the same fashion but with slight variations.

1. Choose your color theme and condition the clay. The whole effect of the cane depends upon the contrast or subtle blending of the colors. You will need two inside colors and an outline color (contrasting). For example, salmon, pale yellow, and white.

2. Start with a large tube of clay, approximately 4" long by 1/2" in diameter.

3. Wrap with an additional color of clay. Make sure the edges meet exactly to create a smooth, even, layer around the core.

4. Wrap with a third ultra-thin layer; this will outline the flower. Note: White outlines will really pop the design out, but be sure the outline has contrast with the main color.

5. Slicing the entire length of the cane, make a center cut about midway through the cane (don't cut all the way through the diameter) (Fig. 1). Insert an ultra-thin sheet and trim at the edge of the cane (Fig. 2). Repeat, cutting two more slices at an angle from the center cut, but not as deep as the first. Insert clay sheets and trim the outside edge. Place a tiny snake of accent clay at the outer location of the slices (Fig. 3).

6. Reduce and pinch this cane into a diamond for assembling into a pattern (Fig. 4).

Fig. 1

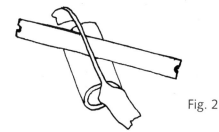

Fig. 2

Fig. 3

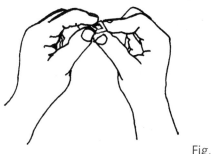

Fig. 4

Rhythm

Whereas pattern is structured repetition of an element, rhythm is the repetition of the visual movement of the elements. It is the flow or the movement of the sequence. This can be expressed with progression (or diminishment) in size or value of an element. Again, nature is a perfect example of rhythm: a fern's fronds diminish in size creating a rhythm, heads of wheat are beautiful patterns that visually lead the eye to the tendrils, and an octopus' tentacles have a rhythmic pattern to their placement.

Right: "All Choked Up" by Nancy Banks of Banks!. The texture of this beautiful organic form flows with rhythm. Banks won an award at the "Moving Forward" exhibit in Bethesda, Maryland, for her work.

Hap Sakwa

"Desert" by Carol L. Simmons. These awesome desert, garden, and seashore scenes mimic the rhythm found in nature.

Sandra McCaw. A beautiful cascade of floral designs creates rhythm with gradation of color and multiple repetitions of form.

Rhythm gives uniformity and cohesiveness. Picture the rhythmic alignment of windows as they line up across the side of a building. Handwriting and calligraphy are a rhythmic linkage of characters. Street and bridge lights are set in rhythmic patterns throughout a city.

Not all rhythms consist of identical or like elements. Variety is the spice of life and a key to keeping interest. A string of beads may be interesting because of the variety in the rhythm of the beads' sizes, shapes, and colors. Books on a shelf create a certain rhythm when each one is a different thickness and height. Weaves in a cloth are interesting because of a variation in the threads. Billows of smoke or flames in a fire can have a rhythm of movement even though each gesture is unique.

Right: "Caught by the Ropes" by Anita Sterling Winthrop, Thumbprints Artwear. The rhythmic loops of the macrame serve to unify this piece.

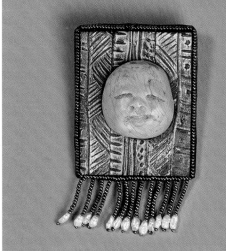

Left: Lizzee Tamayo. Repetitions in line and texture are an excellent illustration of rhythm in this alluring piece.

Opposite page: "Barnacles II" by Cynthia Toops. The line in the design adds variety to the rhythm of this piece.

Opposite page, far right: "Open Look in Loop Chaining" by Nan Roche. Roche creates a rhythmic flow of line by weaving polymer clay. The gradation in color also adds movement to this amazing work.

Roger Schreiber

Chris Roche

Rhythm of the Sea

This project uses a night lamp that was designed by Crooked River Crafts especially for covering with polymer clay. There are many different styles available, or you can use a common candle votive and enjoy the same effects. The lamp in this example was made with transparent Fimo clay #01, because it does not plaque and resembles milk glass. It is recommended that you do a few test bakes of the clay you wish to use in order to understand its transparent qualities after it has been baked. The base shown was covered with Magic Leaf-patterned leaf and was chosen to be in harmony with the seaside design.

Materials

2 blocks transparent white polymer clay
Glass night light or candle votive*
Magic Leaf "Flower"
Magic Leaf adhesive
Magic Leaf Special Varnish
Assorted stamped metal findings of the same theme
Cornstarch, sandpaper, roller, blade, pasta machine
*Style shown designed by Crooked River Crafts. It includes glass, sockets, bulb, and base.

1. Choose several stamped findings that reflect one theme (sea horses and shells were used in this example). It is recommended that they be in a variety of sizes (Fig. 1).

2. Cover the glass lamp or votive with an even layer of conditioned clay, approximately 1/10" thick

3. Dust the entire surface with cornstarch.

4. Press the findings carefully into the surface in an organized sequence on the surface of the piece (Fig. 2). Repeat the pressed images to create a rhythmic pattern. You can also tilt the designs to create a rhythmic movement (Fig. 3).

5. Bake the glass only—do not put the base or wires into the oven. Watch the temperature closely because translucent clays have a tendency to brown; many have a lower recommended baking temperature than other clays.

6. When cooled, trim the edge of the clay to fit the base.

7. To cover the base: Sand the base lightly to roughen the surface. Coat with the adhesive. Apply the Magic Leaf Flower design and cover with varnish.

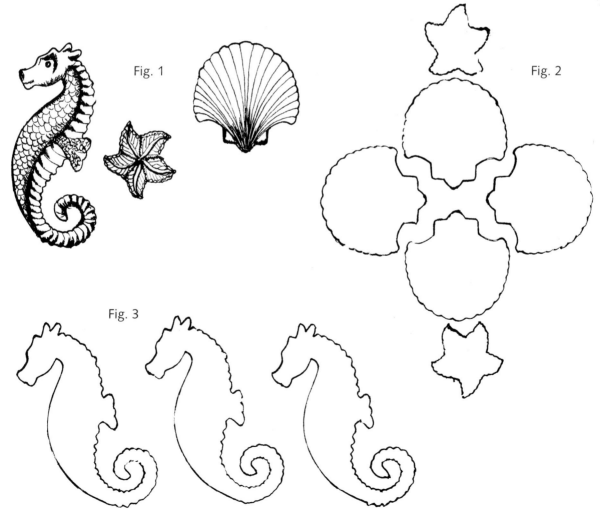

Fig. 1

Fig. 2

Fig. 3

114

Chapter 11

Movement, Contrast, and Emphasis

These principles are the attention-grabbers. While the other principles work to stabilize a piece, contrast, emphasis, and movement are the relationships between the elements that direct attention, lead the eye, and demand notice. It is important to be clear on how they work within a design so they are not overused. Each of these principles helps us to clarify our communication. When your work looks dull or needs a spark, you can count on these principles to make your design come alive.

Mike Buesseler. Elegantly simple applications of line elements move the eye in this unique locket.

Movement

Will Truchon. This bowl illustrates how texture can add movement to a piece. Truchon was successful in developing techniques for throwing polymer clay on a potter's wheel at the 1997 "Making History" conference.

Movement refers to what it sounds like, it moves the eye. If our eye were only drawn to one place within a composition, we would readily tire and might even miss hidden points of interest. Most frequently, our eye begins at the bottom left of a page and works inward. When an object is "hanging off the page" it attracts the attention of our eye. Placement also moves the eye. An obvious placement of emphasis is the middle of something; but if the object is placed elsewhere, it demands our eye to move. It also adds interest by avoiding the obvious. A line is another common way to lead the eye through a design.

Claire Piper, ClairVoy Arts. This cane design uses an object placed at the edge of the composition to create movement, drawing the viewer into the design.

Color is also a way to lead the eye. When something leads us from light to dark, or vice versa, this is referred to as visual passage or linkage. Gradation in shape or color is an obvious way to move the eye, for contrast leads the eye. Repetition in color will also lead the eye.

When you first consider movement, you might think of physical working parts, flowing fabric, or hair. In a design, the art itself is not moving, except in kinetic art such as mobiles, but your eye moves to follow the movement implied by the arrangement of shapes, colors, and lines in the design. The flowing, gestured lines in a dance or a succession of swirling shapes will lead your eye to move directionally. The laces on a ballet slipper lead the eye up the foot. Long flowing hair leads the eye away from the face. The rays of a fan lead the eye outward from the center of the fan and along its edge to return to its base. Our eyes are grateful for the journey and we are satisfied to have captured the complete visual expression.

Ted Brobst

Above: Jane Brobst. The texture and line in Brobst's awesome collection of eggs adds movement to the design.

Below: "Celebration Dance" by Jeanne Sturdevant. Texture and line create movement in this wonderfully energetic sculpture.

Opposite page: Tablet book by Dayle Doroshow. The underlying darker values of color in this tablet book move the eye across the design.

Opposite page, far right: Karen and Ann Mitchell, AnKara Designs. The repeated colors, plus the sequence of beads, moves our eye through this stunning piece.

Hands on Movement

This simple pin is fun to design. It illustrates movement by the repetition of inlaid holographic strips and the graduated mica gold spiral which leads the eye through the composition. The shape of the hand itself leads the eye in and around the fingers. There is enough space in the composition for all of the elements to work together. This composition is completely suggested. It is a good opportunity to experiment with new techniques and clay formulations without getting too serious!

Materials

1/2 block Fimo Soft Special Effects Metallic Blue
Snake of gold clay
1/3 block black clay
Hand cookie cutter, star cookie cutter
Holographic gold transfer foil (a small strip)
Red Fimo pulver
Pin back, straight edge, card stock, varnish (optional), pasta machine

1. Condition the blue clay.

2. Flatten and score a hand shape from the clay, but do not cut out (Fig. 1).

3. Roll a "wedge" snake of gold clay. Set aside (Fig. 2).

4. Cut a star shape from the black clay and coat with red pulver or any surface powder. (Use a protective mask when working with metallic powders.) Set aside.

5. Place a strip of holographic transfer foil (gray side to the clay) on a thin sheet of black clay. Using a straight edge, burnish the foil transfer into the clay. Bake the strip, cut into tiny lengths, and set aside.

6. Compose the piece by placing the prepared surface decorations strategically on top of the hand (Fig. 3).

7. When you have arranged the elements as desired, roll the entire piece smooth, embedding the elements into the surface. Recut the hand shape and remove the scrap from the outline.

8. Place the pin face down on a piece of card stock and attach the pin back with a thin strip of clay.

9. Bake the piece.

10. Varnish if desired.

Fig. 1

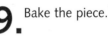

Fig. 2

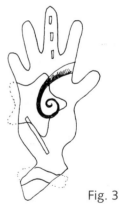

Fig. 3

*C*ontrast

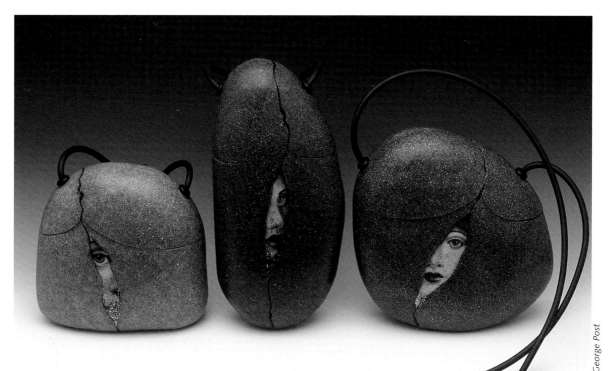

George Post

Contrast is the principle that measures excitement or distinction between things that are different. We distinguish something as being different because of its surroundings. A triangle is in contrast to a group of circles. Jagged lines are in contrast to smooth lines. Details are in contrast with a large surface area.

Above: Kathleen Dustin. The large areas of space are in contrast with the details of the facial images which draw the viewer to the focal point of her work.

Right: Carol Shelton. This dynamic pin employs contrast of value and also of line. The zigzag line contrasts sharply with the smooth line that forms the edge of the pin.

Bill Nieberding

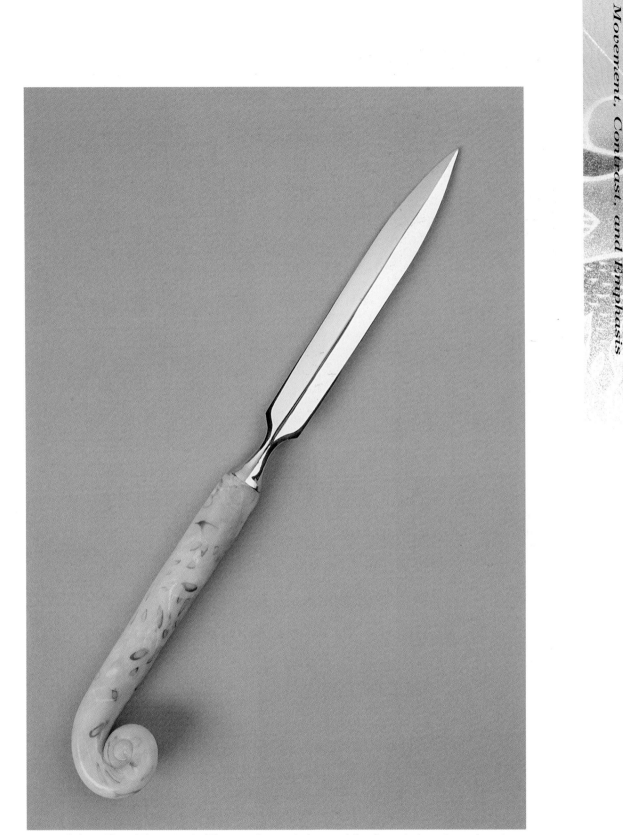

Lois J. Ockner. The subtle contrast of the smooth organic form and the sharp steel create an elegant, intriguing design.

Color has very obvious qualities of contrast. Black text is in stark contrast with white paper, therefore it is clearly noticed. This is referred to as value contrast because it is the extreme difference between light and dark. Color saturation can contrast. A red triangle will stand out on a page of gray triangles. A red circle will stand out in a group of black triangles because the shape and the color are different. More dramatic contrast occurs when an organic shape is placed in a composition with geometric shapes.

Size is another way the artist can add contrast to the elements; in a group of small elements and one large, the contrast in size will draw attention to the large. In fact, all of the elements can be expressed with characters of contrasting nature.

One of the first things children learn to communicate is contrast, or how to differentiate between high and low, thin and thick, big and small, and black and white. Contrast is so common it is often taken for granted. It is obvious we wouldn't want everything to be the same, but we wouldn't want everything to be drastically different either. Contrast can add pleasant interest to a group of things that needs to be somewhat related. Consider the beads in a necklace. The design is more interesting if the beads are somewhat varied; the size and boldness of the beads as individual elements will draw attention to what the designer wants to highlight. But we can overdo it—too extreme or bold contrast can overwhelm the composition. Contrast is a tool we use to execute the purpose of our design. Attention should still remain with the focus of the design, not the contrast itself.

Above: Gwen Gibson. The contrast in texture, created by the use of seed beads, adds interest to these mokume gane earrings. Gibson also employs contrast of size between the earring form and the attached finding.

Opposite page: Pier Voulkos; woodwork by Daniel Peters. Curved legs are a wonderfully simple contrast to the straight lines of the table top.

Diederik Van Heyningen

Above: Petra Nieuwenhuize of Zigzag. The contrast of the black and white draws interest to these bead forms.

Left: Geoffrey McCabe and Darren Listen of Seventh Sense. Contrast of color creates the clarity and definition in this incredible cane work by Seventh Sense.

Tick Tack Contrast

This is a simple game to illustrate contrast in color and shape. It is a study on simultaneous contrast; that is, how a color is influenced by its surrounding colors. Notice how the pieces look, depending on what color they are placed. The triangle shapes also are in slight contrast to the squares. If there were too much contrast, such as making them organic shapes, the piece would not have unity.

Materials

1 block black clay
1/4 block yellow, blue, red, and green clay
Kemper square and triangle punch cutters*
Roller, blade, pasta machine
*You can also cut your own paper square and triangle patterns

1. Condition a flat sheet of base clay. The example shown uses black for its sharp contrast with the bright colors.

2. Using a punch (or paper pattern), cut out the following from flat sheets of conditioned clay (Fig. 1):
• four yellow squares
• five blue squares
• five tiny red triangles
• five tiny green triangles

3. Place the squares as shown on the flat sheet (Fig. 2).

4. Trim the piece with a sharp blade (see Fig. 2).

5. Bake the board piece and the playing pieces.

6. Play like tick tack toe to win! (Fig. 3)

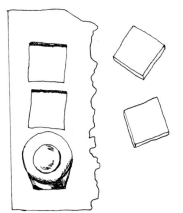

Fig. 1

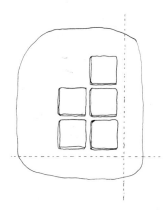

Fig. 2

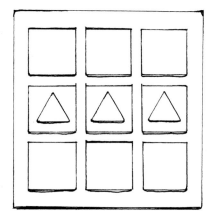

Fig. 3

Emphasis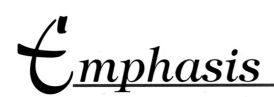

Emphasis creates focus, the main point of communication, in a work. Emphasis is how we use the elements to direct the viewer to that focal point. Placement is an obvious way to emphasize a focal point. If you place an element dead-center, it will be directly emphasized, whereas placing an object off-center will add emphasis to it and still allow the other elements to lead the eye through the rest of the composition.

Differentiation is a way to achieve emphasis. A single tree in the middle of a concrete downtown receives emphasis. Isolation is another way to draw attention, such as an element set apart from a group. Exaggeration—making one aspect of an image larger than the others—also creates emphasis.

"Lips" by Paulette Anderson Thiele. The image of the lips is emphasized in the center placement of this composition; however, the elements of line, color, and texture are strong enough to add interest and movement to this stylish pin.

"The Ogre of the Woods" by Carol Listenberger. The exaggeration of the features of this troll character emphasizes its personality.

Quantity of an image can produce empha-
sis. If you have several types of fruits in an organized group, but mostly apples, the dominance is
on apples. Color dominance is another way to
produce emphasis, especially because color
relates so much to mood.

Too much emphasis can be confusing, over-
whelming, and tiresome. Think of our news
media: when things are continually emphasized,
the instinct is to turn it off. "Emphasizing everything means you've emphasized nothing"
(Ballard and Siebert, *Making a Good Layout*), so
making a good layout emphasis only works when
we are clear in our communication. We must
choose our most important
message. If we are going
to focus on something, we
need to present it without
distraction.

Liv Ames

*Above right: "Shoe Heaven" by
Deborah Anderson. Emphasis is
achieved by repetition of the
forms in Anderson's delightful
necklace.*

*Right: "Enduring Love" by B.
Christine Brashers. The color
and the repeated shape of the
heart provide emphasis to the
theme of in this expressive
work.*

Michael Honer

Angel by Shane Smith. The heavenly emphasis in Smith's work is communicated through the abundant use of white, the soft flowing lines, and the subject matter itself. Attention is drawn to the beautiful basket of flowers by the contrast of using color in that area.

Less is More

This project presents a straight-forward emphasis on the block script which says "Happy New Year" in Chinese. The pin is "framed" in layers of contrasting clay, drawing attention to what's inside the frame. This technique incorporates the fascinating mica shift in certain metallic clay and was disclosed to me by Evelyn Gibson who discovered the effect after experimentation with stamps. The visible edges of the stacked clay form create texture as well as lines around the centerpiece. The form is not an exact square, which makes it a little more interesting. The color choices enhance the cultural association and the value changes in the mica shift create enough contrast to define the calligraphy. The calligraphy featured in the stamp reflects balance, rhythm, and unity. Even though a design may be straight-forward and simple, it still can possess the elements and principles of art.

Materials

Gold Fimo clay with mica shift properties
Three other colors (your choice) of clay; enough to cut a 2" square
Rubber stamp with words or script
400, 600, and 800 grit wet sand paper
Motorized buffing wheel or soft buffing cloth
Cornstarch, soft brush, tissue blade, pin back, card stock, signature cane slice or permanent marker (optional), pasta machine
Note: If you do not wish to buff the piece, it can also be varnished for similar results.

1. Condition and prepare 2" squares (about 1/16" thick) of each color clay. It is important that you condition the gold so that the mica aligns in one direction. Run it several times through a pasta machine or fold and flatten several times consecutively.

2. Lightly dust the stamp with cornstarch.

3. Press the stamp into the gold clay and release the stamp. If you press the stamp with your fingers up into the sheet of clay, you will most likely get a deeper relief (Fig. 1).

Fig. 1

4. Trim the clay with the blade to a "squarish" shape. You can bow the blade slightly to give a discreet curve to the shape.

5. Stack the clay on the next layer of clay. Very carefully shave the very top of the impressed clay, removing the bits of clay that are protruding from the top of the gold clay. You will be shaving off the texture. As you remove the shavings, set them aside (Fig. 2). Continue until the surface is flush, taking care not to shave too deeply, or you will erase the image (Fig. 3).

Fig. 2

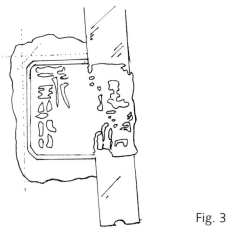

Fig. 3

6. Gently roll the shaved gold surface flush to even out the slight variations on the surface of the clay. This may actually define the mica shift more brilliantly. If the gold square becomes distorted, you can remove it and trim it again.

7. Trim the base layer of clay to a slightly larger square than the gold piece (see dotted lines on Fig. 2).

8. Place the entire work on another layer. Trim again.

9. Place the pin face down on a piece of smooth card stock. Attach a pin back to the back side of the piece by securing the finding to the clay with an additional small square of clay. Add a signature cane slice if available, or sign after baking with a permanent marker (Fig. 4).

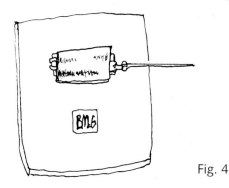

Fig. 4

10. Bake the piece. When the pin is cool, wet-sand by hand with 400, 600, and 800 grit wet sand paper.

11. Polish the pin on a jeweler's buffing wheel or hand polish with a soft cloth.

Variation: By saving the "scraps" you shave off from the gold impressed clay, you can place them (cut side up) on a square of contrasting clay. Roll the clay smooth with a brayer and you have an interesting rendition of the original stamp with which to design.

Personal Journey Journal

In this project, the emphasis is on you! In the journal shown, focus is on the picture. All of the elements are placed to lead the eye toward the picture, while keeping balance with the entire design, and they all relate to the picture. This might not be obvious to the viewer, but as I stated earlier in this book, creativity need only please you! Use your journal to keep a record of ideas, drawings, and quotes.

Materials

Clay
Collect a few things you like or reflect something about you:
• Something for texture, like a favorite button, stamped piece of jewelry, or coin
• Rubber stamp of words, nature, or astrology (Fig. 1)
• A verse, quote, rhyme, or short phrase
• Picture of yourself (enlarged to desired size) (Fig. 2)
• Memento such as a coin, charm, or flat bead (Fig. 3)

Pigment ink or embossing ink and powder
Cornstarch, mica powder, or Fimo pulver
Q-tip or soft brush, metallic pen, tracing paper, colored pencil, small journal, E-6000 glue, pasta machine
Note: When positioning the objects, it is recommended to move them around before you decide upon the final placement (Fig. 4). Each suggestion is variable and may be left out of the composition at your discretion.

1. Using tracing paper, trace the photo using a few lines to suggest the image. With the colored pencil, flip the paper over and again trace the image. Color as desired. This will give you an exact image, not a reverse, to transfer to the clay.

2. Cut a piece of tracing paper the size of the journal. Trim the paper to create a shape for the flat piece of clay that will be positioned on top. Alter it in some way to make it interesting, leaving some blank space on the journal to write the verse.

3. Condition and roll a flat piece of pale-colored clay that complements the theme, approximately 1/8" thick, about the size of the journal. Cut or tear the clay according to the pattern.

4. Transfer the drawn image onto the clay by laying the paper (color side down) directly on the clay. You may trim the paper but do not press on the edges to avoid creating a line or dent in the surface.

5. Coat the button with release powder using a Q-tip or soft brush and press in an area where you would like to have texture. It can be a border, in a pattern or random, or merely an indication of texture. If you use mica powder or pulver as the release powder, the color should be complementary to the journal and clay.

6. Very carefully ink the rubber stamp and apply the impression to the clay. (Apply ink and embossing powder if appropriate. It will cure in the oven.) When you are positioning this element, think of the overall balance of the design.

7. Bake the journal. When it is cool, glue the clay art to the top of the journal. Glue on the momento in a strategic location that will lead the eye through the composition.

8. Finish the composition by writing the verse directly on the journal with the metallic pen. Sign your art.

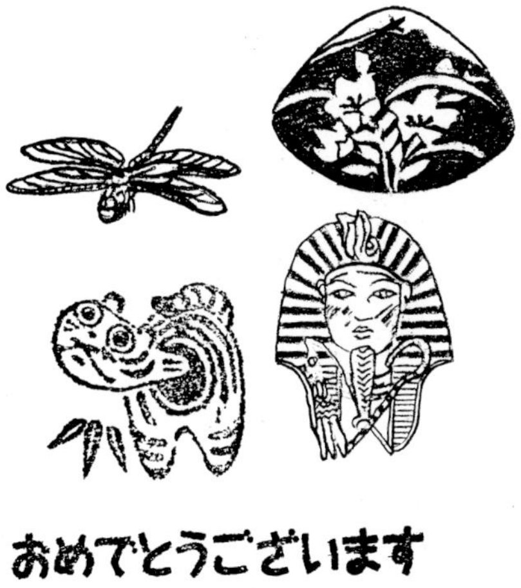

おめでとうございます

Fig. 1

Fig. 2

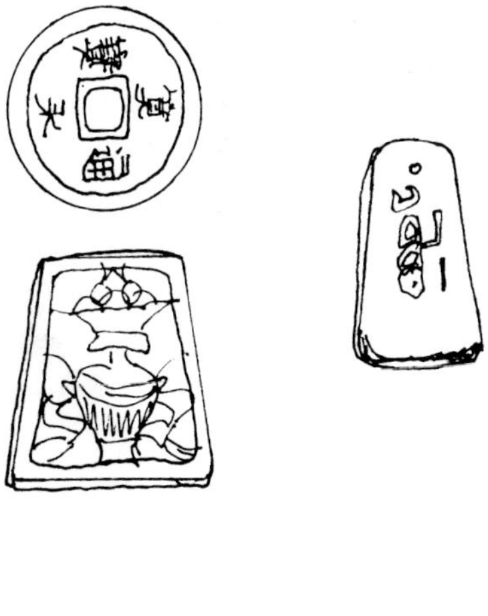

Fig. 3

Fig. 4

Unity

My work used to look like a hodge-podge of all of my favorite things—and it seemed that even if the pieces were made of different images, the look was still the same, a melting pot. This is not unity. Unity can better be introduced as a "sorting station," a group of like objects. What is the common denominator? When I started to eliminate things that really didn't belong in the design, or that I could possibly do without, the unity between the remaining elements was stronger. Space became a much more appreciated element. Each element in itself gained more character. My work had variety and increased quality. I speak of the changes in my own work, because, as I researched the information in the previous chapters, it resulted in a profound improvement in my design. This chapter is placed at the close of the book because it employs the summation of all of the elements. Unity allows the elements to work together as a team and bond the design together as a whole.

"Peeping Face" by Sarajane Helm. Consistent use of organic forms unifies this necklace of shell beads. The subtle colors give a light, arid feeling that complements the delicacy of the elegant image in the centerpiece.

Unity, or harmony, is the principle of how the elements are related to each other in a group. In essence, they should look like they belong together. If a piece is unified, the eye will flow smoothly around the design because the elements are associated to each other. Continuity also describes unity; for example, if the edges of a box were rounded that would support a continuous theme throughout the design. If images or motifs are of the same cultural origin, that may unify a design; it would be odd to place Asian characters on a whimsical checkerboard teapot, because the contrast generally would not complement or be in harmony with the rest of the elements.

It's not to say that unity must be without contrast. Indeed, variation is essential to keep art from being boring. Consider, however, the animal kingdom: animals are one family and there is considerable variety in their differences. Unity can extend to include many elements and references; think of an ocean scene or a city scape. When you dress, it is silly to wear a ski parka, necktie, silk pajamas, and sandals, because those articles of clothing don't go together. They have little to do with each other except that they are clothes and shoes. Choosing elements that support

"Rebirth #3" by Jane Cook. Clustering adds emphasis to the unity of the images in this delightful flute.

your message strengthens the design; when you achieve unity within a design, your message is strengthened.

Color can be a unifying theme. Have you ever seen items grouped together that are all the same color, varying in value, shades, and tints? How about a floral arrangement in yellows, a baby's bedroom done in pinks, or "army green" camping equipment?

Positioning can also be unifying. Clustering objects together can create unity. Repeated shapes, images, and textures will add cohesiveness to a design.

It is not surprising that many talented artists are able to express their entire collection of works with a single unifying style. It comes from the reliance on their intensely personal natures, rich with variety but unified as expressions of their personality. Many of us strive to accomplish this identity and continuity.

Lisa Pavelka. This classic design is unified by the texture of the mosaic.

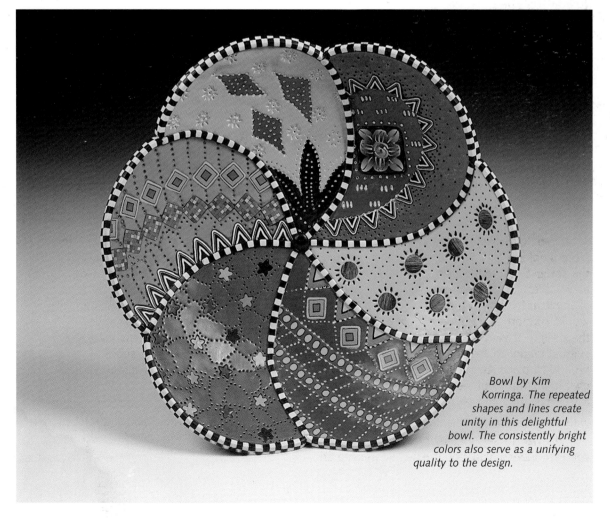

Bowl by Kim Korringa. The repeated shapes and lines create unity in this delightful bowl. The consistently bright colors also serve as a unifying quality to the design.

*S*tamped Expressions

This wall piece uses a limited-edition designer stamp by Commotion—the Art of Rubber Stamping. It was designed by Robert Shields, who is also an incredible artist currently working in polymer clay. All of the elements—the color, texture, images, and line in the cane work—relate to Native Americans. The piece was made to express the dismantling and reassembling of the Indian Peoples.

Materials

2 blocks clay for background
Assorted colors polymer clay
Large rubber stamp image
Acrylic paint, roller, blade, cornstarch, pasta machine
Cane (clay choice should be suitable for caning):
• 1 block middle color
• 1/2 block wrap color, two colors
• 1/4 block black clay for middle line

1. Choose a theme and a rubber stamp image that expresses that theme.

2. Choose and mix clay colors and condition into flat sheets. Cut into strips.

3. Position the strips of clay next to each other, lightly dust the clay with cornstarch, and stamp the image across the strips (Fig. 1).

4. Shift the strips up or down, distorting and breaking apart the image (as arrows indicate in Fig. 1). Trim the strips as desired on the ends, by either tearing or cutting.

5. Position the entire impressed image on an additional background sheet of clay and trim or tear as desired. The clay shown is a combination of translucent and mica particles, which makes it look like quartz.

6. Stack the art on one more bottom sheet of clay and tear or cut the edges as desired. (You can also tear these edges after baking by using a blade to lightly score the border from underneath and tearing along the scores; Fig. 2.)

7. Accent the piece with cane slices (as shown) and found objects if desired (not shown) that relate to the theme. (Directions for zigzag canes shown here are on the following page.)

8. Bake the piece.

9. After the piece has cooled, rub acrylic paint into the stamped image and wipe off the excess. You can lightly sand off the paint after it is dry or use a damp cloth to wipe areas where too much paint has accumulated. In the piece shown, the entire surface was treated in this manner.

10. Frame the piece if desired.

Fig. 1

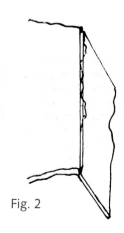

Fig. 2

Zigzag Canes

1. Make a cylinder of clay and wrap it as many times as you like with thin layers of a contrasting color.

2. Reduce it and pinch it into a long, tiny triangle cane.

3. Cut into ten pieces.

4. Prepare a very thin sheet of clay, again in a contrasting color (black is shown).

5. Line up five triangle canes next to each other, points up (Fig. 1; note: Fig. 1-Fig. 3 show only four triangles).

6. Place the sheet of clay next to the triangles, up and down the ridges made by the triangles (Fig. 2).

7. Now insert the remaining triangles, point down, into the valleys of the cane (Fig. 3).

8. Pack the cane together and reduce the pattern to the desired length. You may have some distortion on the ends but the middle will reveal a zigzag pattern running through the cane.

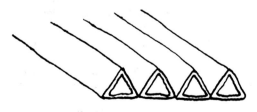

Fig. 1

Fig. 2

Fig. 3

Glossary

The following glossary of polymer clay terms was created with the help of *Webster's Dictionary*, Seventh Edition, *The New Clay*, by Nan Roche, *Color Harmony*, by Hideaki Chijiwa, the *PolyInformer* newsletter, and conversation amongst polymer artists.

Achromatic: Colors without color: white, black, and neutral shades of gray.

Acrylic sheet: A flat sheet of acrylic, variable size or thickness, often used as a work surface.

Analogous colors: Colors next to each other on the color wheel.

Appliqué: Applied on top of.

Armature: A skeletal framework used as a structural support.

Block: A small 2-ounce unit of polymer clay.

Brayer: A roller tool that has a handle for leverage and increased pressure. Acrylic brayers are suitable for work with polymer clay because an artist can see the surface while rolling.

Brick: A large 13-ounce unit of Fimo.

Buffing wheel: A machine-driven wheel that has a muslin or flannel disk used for buffing. Drill pads with muslin bonnets, which can also shine polymer surfaces, are also available.

Bull's eye: A design of circles, increasing in diameter and graduating outward from the same midpoint.

Burnisher: A tool with a flat, blunt wand used to smooth or shine an area using friction.

Cane: A cylinder or length (any shape) of clay (or glass) wherein several rods or sheets of color have been placed together to form a design running lengthwise through the shape.

Clay extruder: A hand-operated tool that presses clay through an opening to extrude the clay in a continuous shape.

Conditioning: The preparation of polymer clay before use. Polymer clay must be kneaded or made pliable before use to allow the molecules in the clay to align properly for stretching.

Convection oven: An oven that heats with a continuous flow of air. This is particularly favorable when even and exact heating is desired.

Crimp bead: A tiny metal bead that clamps flat to hold wire by pressure.

E-6000: Name brand of a strong, water-resistant silicate base glue.

Embossing powder: Powder used in rubber stamp design. When heat-treated it will become a shiny solid and rise slightly above the stamped surface.

Eye pin: A long, straight, rigid metal wire with a loop at one end used in connecting beads or jewelry findings.

Harmony: In color; an acetic arrangement of parts to form a pleasing whole.

Head pin: A straight wire pin with a nail head used in connecting components of jewelry; usually an end unit that dangles.

Fimo modeling material: Polymer clay modeling material manufactured by Eberhard Faber, GmbH, Germany.

Findings: Components used in making jewelry; usually refers to the mechanical apparatus.

Food processor: A motorized chopper intended for food but can be used to condition polymer clay.

Glow in the dark: Fluorescent or colors that glow under a black light.

Gold leaf: An extremely thin sheet of imitation metal similar to a foil. Leafing comes in several colors, including gold, silver, and variegated.

Graduated beads: Beads that increase or decrease in size in equal proportions.

Grit: Coarseness of texture in sanding papers or powders.

Guild: A group or association of kindred pursuits or having a common interest.

Hue: The actual color.

Inlay: A decorative inlaid pattern.

Intaglio: An engraving depressed below the surface of a material so that an impression from the design yields an image in relief.

Lacquer: A surface coating that dries as a protective finish, gloss, or matte over an object.

Lamination: The process of uniting superposed layers of one or more materials.

Latex gloves: Thin stretchable gloves (commercial or medical) used to protect hands and prevent fingerprints from imprinting on a piece.

Loaf: A cane; a long square shape that will eventually be sliced.

Log: A cylindrical cane or shape of clay.

Marbleizing: The mixing of two or more colors of clay to produce a streaked or marbled effect resembling stone.

Millefiori: Refers to a process developed by Venetian glass makers where several rods of glass are fused together in a pattern (often star or floral). Pieces of the resulting designed cane are then applied to the surface of another piece of glass or used in lengths crosswise, exposing the design. In Italian it literally means "Thousand Flowers."

Mokume gane: A Japanese metal smithing technique that is currently popular in polymer clay. Layers of clay (and leaf) are altered by pushing up or sinking objects or clay into the layers to create positive/negative special relations. When the layers are sliced horizontally, the "terrain" of the clay resembles rings or patterns as the artist altered the layered clay.

Molds: The negative relief impression of an object, wherein another piece of clay may be pressed and the original design is duplicated.

Monochromatic: Colors made from tints and shades of the same hue.

Onlay: Applying a piece of clay onto another piece of clay.

Opaque: Neither reflecting nor emitting light; not transparent or translucent.

Parchment paper: Oven baking paper that is used when baking polymer clay to eliminate "shiny spots" on pieces.

Pasta machine: A mechanical device intended to roll pasta but used in the polymer clay industry to condition, blend color, texturize, and roll clay into flat sheets of varying thickness.

Pearlescent: Having a shimmering quality; clay that includes a non-metallic filler that reflects microscopic bits of light and sparkles softly.

Photocopy transfer: The transferring of an image printed on a photocopier and then applied to polymer clay in a technique that transfers the ink and subsequently the image to the clay.

Plasticizer: The chemical agent that enables softness or initial consistency to polymer clay.

Polymer: A chemical compound of high molecular weight consisting of many small molecules linked in a chain.

Polymer clay: A modern modeling material composed primarily of PVC resin, plastizer, and occasional filler material. It is a colorful clay-like modeling compound that is cured at a temperature of 265° F and is permanent and water resistant.

Polyvinyl chloride: Commonly known as PVC, a polymerized vinyl chloride compound, thermoplastic resin.

Pulver: Micro-metallic powder used to coat polymer clay with a metallic sheen.

Reduction: The shrinking of a design pattern to a smaller scale. Usually refers to a cane that is created in a large scale and then reduced in proportion by various techniques.

Resilience: The capability of a strained body to recover its size and shape after deformation by comparative stress.

Saturation: Vividness or intensity of a color.

Shade: Darkness of a color; the amount of black mixed with a hue.

Skinner process: A technique in which colored clay is folded and pressed to meld into a smooth gradation of one color to another.

Snake: A roll or cylinder of clay.

Spiral: A "Jelly Roll" design in a cane where sheets of clay are stacked and rolled to create a spiral design when sliced crossways.

Stone Fimo: Refers to the colors of a brand of Fimo modeling material simulating stone.

Swap: Trade; an event popular amongst Internet members where a large group of artists simultaneously exchanges pieces of a particular theme.

Tensil strength: Strength relating to capability of tension.

Tint: Lightness of a color; the amount of white mixed with a hue.

Tissue blade: An extremely sharp, smooth blade borrowed from the medical industry that has the ability to slice thin, precise layers.

Toggle clasp: A clasp that has a "T" shape inserted into an opening (round or otherwise) to catch and hold two strands.

Translucent: Shining or glowing through; admitting and diffusing light so that objects beyond cannot be clearly distinguished. When referring to Fimo-00 Art Translucent, the sheerest clay, which when used in thin layers or buffed is almost clear.

Transparent: Having the property of transmitting light without appreciable scattering so that bodies beyond are visible. When referring to Fimo, it is similar to porcelain, having a soft depth but not clear.

Value: The degree of lightness or darkness in a color.

Varnish: The coating or covering applied to an object; a protective surface material.

Artist Directory

Christine Alibert
3 rue descente du Portal
34150 Saint-Guilhem-Le Desert
France
33-4-67-57-31-87
alibert@club-internet.fr

Deborah Anderson
265 N.13th St.
San Jose, CA 95112-3445
408-998-5303
maraha@aol.com

Maggie Ashton
Box 265
Greensboro, PA 15338
724-943-4944
riverrun@greenepa.net

Nancy Banks
Banks!
627 Orvis Ave.
San Jose, CA 95112
408-279-5144

Joanne Bañuelos
3238 Fallen Oak Ct.
San Jose, CA 95148
408-274-5368
JBanuelos@laserscope.com

Sonja Diana Barrios
7458 Rush River Dr. #710-289
Sacramento, CA 95831
JoeEB@att.net

Edward Bednar, see Two Bent Fish, page 143

Toni Belonogoff
2219 43rd Ave.
San Francisco, CA 94116
415-564-3939

Linda Bernstein
Lbernstein@Artique.org

Jody Bishel
548 Wakelee Ave.
Ansonia, CT 06401-1226
dbuck16803@aol.com

B. Christine Brashers
8976 Foothill Blvd. #437
Rancho Cucamonga, CA 91730
909-989-2453
chrissyfri@aol.com

Martha Breen
510-839-9798

Jane Brobst
2702 Woodbreeze
Drive Cantonment, FL 32533
850-484-8468

Mike Buesseler
2312 59th St. Ct. NW
Gig Harbor, WA 98335
rae@narrows.com

Dotty Calabrese
Just for Fun
P.O. Box 1136
Palo Alto, CA 94302
Dotty@aol.com

Jane Cook
3687 Cedar Run Rd.
Bonne terre, MO 63628
573-431-0077
jcook@socket.net

Dan Cormier
Bead Man Dan
2511 Tyee Dr. RRI Site 24 C67
Gabriola Island BC, Canada
VOR 1XO
250-247-8070
hoco@island.net

Terry Lee Czechowski
7 Sevilla Dr.
Cliften Park, NY 12065
518-383-3769
tlccreations@prodigy.net

Cheryl Darrow, see Uptown Rubber Stamps, page 143

Debra Donovan
Commotion
2711 E. Elvira Rd.
Tucson, AZ 85706
520-297-6545
commotion@commotion.com

Dayle Doroshow
P.O. Box 826
Brisbane, CA 94005
415-468-0636

Cassie Doyon
99 Brown Street
Tewksbury, MA 01876
cmdoyon99@aol.com

Nuchi Draiman
6134 N. St. Louis Ave.
Chicago, IL 60659
Bdrai@aol.com

Diane Dunville
Illuminart
15309 Moysonike
Court Lanexa, VA 23089
804-966-5756
DMDUNVILLE@aol.com

Kathleen Dustin
4405 Cynthia St.
Bellaire, TX 77401-5636
713-665-8454
dustin@compuserve.com

Celie Fago
RR1 Box 376
Bethel, VT 05032
802-234-5428
vfago@aol.com

Janet Farris
From the Heart
635 Windsor Run
Resno, CA 93726-4423
209-227-7197
jrt20@lennon.csufresno.edu

Jeni Fiske
158 Rhode
Petaluma, CA 94952
707-762-5184
jfiske5324@aol.com

Audrey Forcier, see
Colorado Card & Curiosity,
page 143

Steven Ford/David Forlano
City Zen Cane
1714 N. Mascher St. 3rd Fl
Philadelphia, PA 19122
215-739-0609

Emi Fukushima
785 Sequoia Drive
Sunnyvale, CA 94086
408-738-1869
ecreations@aol.com

Evelyn Gibson
1019 Bermuda Dr.
Concord, CA 94518
925-671-2604
gibsonweb@aol.com

Gwen Gibson
216 Bayview
San Rafael, CA 94901
415-454-3246
gwen@mariunterserv.com

Chris Gluck
Wireart
15 Poker Hill Rd.
Underhill, VT 05489
802-899-4483

Michael Grove
Grove & Grove
2510 Russell #3
Berkeley, CA 94705
510-841-3976
www.groveandgrove.com

Lindly Haunani
7630 Tomlinson Ave. #30
Cabin John, MD 20818
LindleyH@aol.com

Amelia Helm
8312 Cedarbrake
Houston, TX 77055
713-461-9513
phelm44115@aol.com

Sarajane Helm
715 Goss Dr.
Longmont, CO 80501
303-684-9069
sjpolyclay@aol.com

Tory Hughes
719 Alondra Lane NW
Albuquerque, NM 87114
505-792-2507

Susan Hyde
100 W. Olympic Pl. #102
Seattle, WA 98119-4750
206-281-1559
shdzclay@aol.com

Marie Johannes
635 Windsor Run
Bloomfield Hills, MI 48304
Eiramjoh@aol.com

Donna Kato, see Prairie
Craft, page 143

Partricia Kimle
3222 Lettle St.
Ames, IA 40014
515-292-3845
pattikimle@kimledesigns.com

Kazuyo Kono
7-8-10-203 Tsukiji Chuo-ku
Tokyo 1040045 Japan 20004
kykaz@aol.com

Kim Korringa
156 Eldora Dr.
Mountain View, CA 94041
650-969-1790
kimcreates@aol.com

Susan Kraus
4113 Lover's Lane
Dickinson, TX 77539
281-337-3073

Margaret Kristof
P.O. Box 882
Fairfax, CA 94978
415-464-1184
kristof@itsa.ucsf.edu

Debbie Krueger
27426 Dobbin-Hufsmith Rd.
Manolia, TX 77354-4001
281-356-8541
dbriank@aol.com

Violette Laporte
1575 desGrands Ducs
Chicoutimi, Quebec,
Canada G7#5J8
418-549-4372
vlaporte@saglac.qc.ca

Margi Laurin
Box 676 KOCIXO
Morrisburg, Ontario, Canada
613-543-2835
mornet64@mor-net.on.ca

Varda Levram-Ellisman
427 N. Rios Ave.
Solana Beach, CA 92075
619-481-2959
vera@alex.ucsd.edu

Karen Lewis, see Klew
Expressions, page 143

Laura Liska
P.O. Box 948
Sonoma, CA 95476-0948
707-939-1236
103272.1174@compuserve.
com

Carole Listenberger
2802 Ferguson Rd.
Ft. Wayne, IN 46809
219-747-0293
ddl52@aol.com

Margaret Maggio
1454 SE 57th
Portland, OR 97215
503-236-7042
maggiomc@aol.com

Geoffrey McCabe/Darren
Lisiten
7nth Sense
151 Merrick Ave.
Merrick, NY 11566

Sandra McCaw
HC 63 Box 53
Alstead, NH 03602
603-835-6408
smccaw@topmonad.net

Barbara A. McGuire
1365 Taylor St. #4
San Francisco, CA 94108
415-922-6366
stylefimo@aol.com

Linda E. Merrill
1259 Cornell Ave.
Berkeley, CA 94706-2307
510-524-4637

Karen and Ann Mitchell
AnKara Designs
260 S. Lake Ave. #158
Pasadena, CA 91101
818-798-8491

Karen Murphy, see
Artifactory, page 142

Petra Nieuwenhuize, see
Zigzag, page 143

Lois J. Ockner
617 Princeton Gate Dr.
Chesterfield, MO 63017
314-227-2210
lois0my@aol.com

Sharon Ohlhorst
5080 West 3400 South
Wellsville, UT 84339
solhusrt@weber.edu

Nancy Osbahr
Checkered Heart Studio
1215 Belleview Dr.
Fort Collins, CO 80526
ckhearts@frii.com

Lisa Pavelka
9825 Tarzana Lane
Las Vegas, NV 98117
702-243-6564
cornman@vegas.infi.net

Claire Piper
Claire Voy Arts
307 Hynes
West Plains, MO 65775
417-256-0706
spirit_1@hotmail.com

Shauna Poong
1337 Club Lane El
Sobrante, CA 94803
510-262-0202
fspg@itsa.ucsf.edu

Carolyn Potter
1759 Putney Rd
Pasadena, CA 91103-1142
818-793-2804
cpotter@ucla.edu

Margaret Regan
416 Miller
Helena, MT 59601
406-443-1149
mregan@mt.net

Nan Roche
4511 Amherst Rd.
College Park, MD 20740
301-864-1805
roche@helix.nih.gov

Karen L. Scudder
8412 Oakfort Dr.
Springfield, VA 22152
703-569-7640
downtowncs@aol.com

Marie Segal, see Clay
Factory, page 142

Carol Shelton
P.O. Box 141379
Columbus, OH 43214-6379
614-267-7593
Argileux@aol.com

Sarah Shriver
8 Redding Way San
Rafael, CA 94901-5238
415-456-7335

Carol L. Simmons
4900 E. Ridge Drive
Ft. Collins, CO 80526-4614
970-229-0370
csim@frii.com

Shelia Sinclair
34 Crestwood
Trophy Club, TX 76262
817-430-9094

Judith Skinner, see JASI,
page 143

Shane Smith
10646 South Highway 67
Sedalia, CO 80135-9506
303-647-2347

Virginia Sperry
Winter Moon Designs
P.O. Box 2241
Elliot City, MD 21041-2241
410-418-4176
vvswmd@hotmail.com

Anita Sterling-Winthrop
Thumbprints Design
926 S. Meridian Rd.
Meridian, CA 95957
530-696-2171
clayaddict@hotmail.com

Jeanne Sturdevant
3600 Highmeadow Drive
Greenville, TX 75402
903-450-0234
jeannest@cyberramp.net

Lizzee Tamayo
2926 Holyrood Dr.
Oakland, CA 94611
510-530-7249
lizzet@aol.com

Paulette Anderson Thiele
Pan der Sont Studio
P.O. Box 2416
Redway, CA 95560
707-923-3392
rontiel@aol.com

Linnea Tobias
P.O. box 1315
Mendocino, CA 95460
707-937-4557

Cynthia Toops
2514 E. Spring St.
Seattle, WA 98122
206-325-4035

Will Truchon
3420 52nd Ave. Apt. #3408
Red Deer
Alberta Canada T4N6N2
403-346-9714

Luann Udell
Durable Goods
312 Walnut St.
Keene, NH 03431
603-358-1056
durablegoods@monad.net

Pier Voulkos
1250-57th Ave. #24
Oakland, CA 94621
510-533-8112
pier4dan@aol.com

Svetlana Vovina
2640 Dole St., #E-201
Honolulu, HI 96822
808-949-8464
vovin@hawaii.edu

Patricia Weller
Morning Dove Design
6703 S. River Rd.
Olathe, CO 81425
970-323-5275
morningdove@aol.com

Elise Winters
56 Adams Street
Haworth, NJ 076411406
wintersE@aol.com

A. Ping L. Yeh
4998 Harmony Way
San Jose, CA 95130
408-374-6720

Carol Steinman Zilliacus
Paint Brush Studio
13303 Collingwood Terrace
Silver Spring, MD 20904
301-236-4395
carolz@concentric.net

Rebecca Zimmerman
2331 North 65th St.
Wauwatosa, WI 53213
414-774-9949

Resources

Accent Import-Export, Inc.
1501 Loveridge Rd.
Box 16
Pittsburg, CA 94565
925-431-1150
www.fimozone.com
**Fimo and Fimo Soft, large
brick clay, Magic Leaf
Patterned leaf, bone
burnishers, rollers**

Almac Camera
445 Stockton St.
San Francisco, CA 94108
415-986-6327
Art photography

American Art Clay Co.
4717 W. 16th St.
Indianapolis, IN 46222
800-372-1600
**Clay, WifeForm mesh,
Genesis paints**

Artifactory
2808 E. Madison
Seattle, WA 98112
206-322-9233
artifactory@juno.com
Clay, classes, workshops

Artistic Wire
1210 Harrison Ave.
La Grange Park, IL 60526
630-530-7567
artwire97@aol.com
Colored wire, all guages

Bead & Button Magazine
Kalmbach Publishing Co.
P.O. Box 1612
Waukesha, WI 53187-1612
414-796-8776
Crafts publication

Clay Factory
750 Citracado Pkwy #21
Escondido, CA 92029
800-243-3455
www.clayfactoryinc.com
**Preemo, Cernit, Jaquard
powers**

Colorado Card & Curiosity
305 W. Main St.
Trinidad, CO 81082
800-789-6221
www.coloradocard.com
Clay art cards

Commotion
2711 E. Elvira Rd.
Tucson, AZ 87506
520-740-0515
commotion@commotion.com
Designer rubber stamps

Crooked River Crafts
413 Main St.
LaFarge, WI 54639
Polymer clay lamp base, Claymates, beads, polymer clay supplies

Designer Editions Creative Claystamps
Barbara McGuire
www.claystamps.com
Positive/negative stamps for clay

Eberhard Faber GmbH
Postfach 1220
92302 Neumarkt Germany
Manufacturer of Fimo clay

Embellishments
7660 Woodway Ste 550
Houston, TX 77063
713-781-6864
shows@quilts.com
National bead show

Flexible Fotography
P.O. Box 654
La Jolla, CA 92038
619-277-2666
Location art photography

Gameplan Artranch
2233 McKinley Ave.
Berkeley, CA 94703
510-549-0993
gameplan@earthlink.net
Instructional videos

George Post Photography
5835 Bouquet Ave.
Richmond, CA 94805
510-237-0197
Art photography

Gold Leaf & Metallic Powders
6001 Santa Monica Blvd.
Los Angeles, CA 90038
323-469-0805
www.GLandMP.com

Metallic powders
Jacuard-Rupert Gibbon & Spider, Inc.
P.O. Box 425
Healdsburg, CA 95448
800-442-0455
www.jacquardproducts.com
Pearlescent powders

JASI
P.O. Box 40219
Pasadena, CA 91114
626-794-1530
members.aol.com/polyannie
Special slicing tool

Jewelry Crafts Magazine
4880 Market St.
Ventura, CA 93003
512-479-7644
Crafts publication

Kemper Tools
13595 12th Street
Chino, CA 91710
714-627-6191
Tools and cutters

Klew Expressions
435 W. J St. I
Tehechapi, CA 93561
805-822-5539
klew@lightspeed.com
Polymer clay, metal art clay, lessons

Krause Publications
700 E. State St.
Iola, WI 54990-0001
715-445-2214
www.krause.com
Publishers of craft books and magazines

Lapidary Journal
60 Chestnut Ave.
Devon, PA 19333
Jewelry and gem publication

Micheal Leonard
Flexible Photography
P.O. Box 654
La Jola, CA 92038
619-277-2666
Location art photography

Limited Edition Rubber Stamps
1514 Stafford St.
Redwood City, CA 94063
877-9STAMPS
www.limitededitionrs.com

Creative clay stamps
Mindstorm Productions
2625 Alcatraz Ave. Ste. 357
Berkeley, CA 94705
800-400-7099
Instructional videos

Munro-Avante
3954 12 Mile Rd.
Berkeley, MI 48072
800-638-0543
Suppliers, general crafts

National Polymer Clay Guild
1350 Beverly Rd. Ste 115-345
Mclean, VA 22101
202-895-5212
www.npcg.org
Polymer clay association

Ornament Magazine
230 Keystone Way
Vista, CA 92083
619-599-0222
Wearable art publication

Polyform Products
1901 Estes Elk
Grove Village, IL 60007
847-427-0020
www.sculpey.com
Manufacturers of polymer clay, Sculpey, Preemo

Polymer Express
800-844-0138
www.polyexp.com
Mail order clay supplies

Prairie Craft
800-779-0615
www.prairiecraft.com
Mail order clay supplies

Ready Stamp
10405 San Diego Mission Rd.
San Diego, CA 92108
619-282-8723
Custom rubber stamps

Rings & Things
P.O. Box 450
Spokane, WA 99210
800-366-2156
Wholesale jewelry supplies

Rio Grande
6901 Washington NE
Albuquerque, NM 87109
800-545-6566
Lapidary and jewelry supplies

Stanislaus Imports
41 Fourteenth St.
San Francisco, CA 94103
415-431-4365
Supplier for general crafts

Two Bent Fish (TBF)
P.O. Box 80126
Phoenix, AZ 85060
800-492-0806
Wholesale clay supplies

TSI
101 Nickerson St.
Seattle, WA 98109
800-426-9984
Jewelry-making supplies, polymer clay

Uptown Rubber Stamps
315 W. Hickory St.
Fort Collins, CO 80524
Rubber stamps, lessons

Wee Folks
18476 Natchez Ave.
Prior Lake, MN 55372-9700
612-447-3828
weefolk@weefolk.com
Clay supplies, seminars by clay artist Maureen Carlson

Zigzag
Petra Nieuwenhuize
8 Cherry Place
Casebrook, Christchurch, New Zealand
3592989
Zigzag polymer clay supplies

Bibliography

Allen, Jamey D. *Five Artists, Five Directions in Polymer Clay*. Gaithersburg, MD: Flower Valley Press. 1995.

Anderson, Arthur D. *A Designer's Notebook*. Bloomington, IN: McKnight and McKnight Publishing Co. 1966.

Bang, Molly. *Picture This, Perception and Composition*. Bulfinch Press, Little Brown and Co. USA. 1991.

Bowen Ballinger, Louise and Thomas F. Vroman. *Design Sources and Resources*. New York: Reinhold Publishing Corporation. 1965.

Brown Ashcroft, Pierette and Lindley Haunani. *Artists at Work*. Rockville, MD: Flower Valley Press. 1996.

Chijiwa, Hideaki. *Color Harmony: A Guide to Creative Color Combinations*. Rockport, MA: Rockport Publishers. 1987.

The Design Concepts Series, Davis Publications, Inc. Worcester, MA 1974–5
Space, Movement and Rhythm by Gerald F. Brommer
Emphasis, Color and Value by Joseph A. Gatto
Texture, Balance and Unity by George F. Horn
Pattern, Shape and Form by Albert W. Porter
Line and Contrast by Jack Selleck

Doczi, Gyorgy. *The Power of Limits, Proportional Harmonies in Nature, Art and Architecture*. Boston: Shambhala Publications, Inc. 1981.

Eitner, Lorenz. *Introduction to Art*. Minneapolis, MN: Burgess Publishing Company.

Ford, Steven and Leslie Dierks. *Creating with Polymer Clay*. Asheville, NC: Lark Books. 1996.

Horth, F. A.C. Coll. H. F. R. S. A. *Design and Handicraft*. Bath, England: Sir Isaac Pitman and Sons, LTD. 1932.

Logic and Design in Art Science and Mathematics. Krome Barratt Design Books, USA. 1980.

O'Hara, Eliot. *Art Teachers' Primer*. New York: Minton, Balch and Co. 1939.

Pearson, Ralph M. *The New Art Education*. New York: Harper and Brothers Publishers. 1941.

Peterson, Bryan L. *Using Design Basics to Get Creative Results*. Cincinnati, OH: North Light Books. 1996.

Proctor, Richard M. *Principles of Pattern Design*. Litton Educational Publishing Inc. New York, Van Nostrand Reinhold. 1969.

Richards, Kris. *New Ways with Polymer Clay*. Iola, WI: Krause Publications. 1997.

Roche, Nan. *The New Clay*. Rockville, MD: Flower Valley Press. 1991.

Russel, M.S., Mable and Elsie Pearl Wilson, M. S. *Art Training through Home Problems*. Peoria, IL: The Manual Arts Press.

Siebert, Lori and Lisa Ballard. *Making a Good Layout*. Cincinnati, OH: North Light Books. 1992.

Sneum, Gunnar. *Teaching Form and Design*. New York: Reinhold Publishing Corporation. 1965.

Wong, Wucius. *Principles of Form and Design*. New York: Van Nostrand Reinhold 1993.

Index